Contents

ONE

Sources of Happiness

Women can be wonderfully happy. When they're in love, when someone gives them flowers, when they've finally found the right pair of shoes and they even fit. I remember once, in love and properly loved, dancing round a room singing, *'They can't take this away from me.'* I remember holding the green shoes with the green satin ribbon (it was the sixties) to my bosom and rejoicing. I remember my joy when the midwife said, *'But this is the most beautiful baby I've ever seen. Look at him, he's golden!'*

The wonderful happiness lasts for ten minutes or so. After that little niggles begin to arise. *'Will he think I'm too fat?' 'Are the flowers his way of saying goodbye?' 'Do the shoes pinch?' 'Will his allegedly separated wife take this away from me?' 'Is solitary dancing a sign of insanity?' 'How come I've produced so wonderful a baby— did they get the name tags wrong?'*

Anxiety and guilt come hot on the heels of happiness. So the brutal answer to what makes women happy is *'Nothing, not for more than ten minutes at a time.'* But the perfect ten minutes are worth living for, and the almost perfect hours that circle them are worth fighting for, and examining, the better to prolong them.

3

Ask women what makes them happy and they think for a minute and come up with a tentative list. It tends to run like this, and in this order:

Sex

Food

Friends

Family

Shopping

Chocolate

'Love' tends not to get a look in. Too unfashionable, or else taken for granted. 'Being in love' sometimes makes an appearance. 'Men' seem to surface as a source of aggravation, and surveys keep throwing up the notion that most women prefer chocolate to sex. But personally I suspect this response is given to entertain the pollsters. The only thing you can truly know about what people think, feel, do and consume, some theorize, is to examine the contents of their dustbins. Otherwise it's pretty much guesswork.

There are more subtle pleasures too, of course, which the polls never throw up. The sense of virtue when you *don't* have an éclair

4

can be more satisfactory than the flavour and texture of cream, chocolate and pastry against the tongue. Rejecting a lover can give you more gratification than the physical pleasures of love-making. Being right when others are wrong can make you very happy indeed. We're not necessarily nice people.

Some women I know always bring chocolates when they're invited to dinner—and then sneer when the hostess actually eats one. That's what I mean by 'not nice'.

Sources of Unhappiness

We are all still creatures of the cave, although we live in loft apartments. Nature is in conflict with nurture. Anxiety and guilt cut in to spoil the fun as one instinct wars with another and with the way we are socialized. Women are born to be mothers, though many of us prefer to not take up the option. *The baby cries; we go. The man calls; 'Take me!' we cry.* Unless we are very strong indeed, physiology wins. We bleed monthly and the phases of the moon dictate our moods. We are hardwired to pick and choose amongst men when we are young, aiming for the best genetic material available. The 'love' of a woman for a man is nature's way of keeping her docile and at home. The 'love' of a man for a woman is protective and keeps him at home as long as she stays helpless. (If high-flying women, so amply able to look after themselves, are so often single, it can be no surprise.)

Or that is one way of looking at it. The other is to recognize that we are moral creatures too, long for justice, and civilized ourselves out of our gross species instincts long ago. We like to think correctly and behave in an orderly and socially aware manner. If sometimes we revert, stuff our mouths with goodies, grab what we can so our neighbour doesn't get it (*'Been to the sales lately?'*) or fall upon our best friend's boyfriend when left alone in the room with him, we feel ashamed of ourselves. Doing what comes naturally does not sit well with modern woman.

And so it is that in everyday female life, doubts, dilemmas and anxieties cut in, not grandiose whither-mankind stuff, just simple things such as:

Sex: *'Should I have done it?'*

Food: *'Should I have eaten it?'*

Friends/family: *'Why didn't I call her?'*

Shopping: *'Should I have bought it?'*

Chocolate: *'My God, did I actually eat all that?'*

But you can't lie awake at night worrying about these things. You have to get up in the morning and work, so you do. But the voice of conscience, otherwise known as the voice of guilt, keeps up its nagging undercurrent. It drives some women to therapists in their attempt to silence it. But it's better to drive into a skid than try to steer out of it. If you don't want to feel guilty, don't do it. If you want to be happy, try being good.

What Makes Men Happy

Men have their own list when it comes to sources of happiness. 'The love of a good woman' is high in the ratings. Shopping and chocolate don't get much of a look in. Watching porn and looking at pretty girls in the street, if men are honest, feature large. These fondnesses of theirs (dismissed by women as 'addictions') can make women unhappy, break up marriages and make men wretched and secretive because the women they love get upset by them.

Women should not be upset. They should not expect men to behave like women. Men are creatures of the cave too. Porn is sex in theory, not in practice. It just helps a man get through the day. And many a woman too, come to that.

Porn excites to sex, sure. Sex incited by porn is not bad, just different. Tomorrow's sex is always going to be different from today's. In a long-term partnership there is room and time for all kinds. Sex can be tender, loving, companionable, a token of closeness and respect, the kind women claim to like. Then it's romantic, intimate, and smacks of permanence. Sometimes sex is a matter of lust, release, excitement, anger, and the sense is that any woman could inspire it. It's macho, anti-domestic. Exciting. Don't resist the mood—try and match it. Tomorrow something else will surface more to your liking. Each sexual act will have a different feel to it, the two instincts in both of you being in variable proportions from night to night, week to week, year to year. It's rare for a couple's sexual energies to be exactly matched. But lucky old you if they are.

I have friends so anxious that they can't let the man in their life out of their sight in case he runs off with someone else. It's counter-productive. Some girls just do stop traffic in the street. So it's not you—so what? Men like looking at pretty girls in the street not because they long to sleep with them, or because given a choice between them and you they'd choose them, but because it's the instinct of the cave asserting itself. Pretty girls are there to be looked at speculatively by men and, if they have any sense, with generous appreciation by women. It's bad manners in men, I grant you, to do it too openly, especially if the woman objects, but not much worse than that.

This will not be enough, I know, to convince some women that for a husband or lover to watch porn is not a matter for shock-horror. But look at it like this. A newborn baby comes into the world with two urgent appetites: one is to feed, the other is to suck. Because the nipple is there to satisfy both appetites, the feeding/sucking distinction gets blurred for both mother and baby. If you are lucky, the baby's time at the breast or bottle is time enough to satisfy the sucking instinct. If you're not lucky, the baby, though fed to completion, cries, chafes and vomits yet goes on sucking desperately, as if it were monstrously hungry. At which point the wise mother goes to fetch a dummy, so everyone can get some peace. Then baby can suck, digest and sleep, all at the same time, blissfully. (Most babies simply toss the dummy out of the cot as soon as they're on solids and the sucking reflex fades, thus sparing the mother social disgrace.)

In the same way, in males, the instinct for love and the need for sexual gratification overlap but do not necessarily coincide. The capacity for love seems inborn; lust weighs in powerfully at puberty. The penis is there to satisfy both appetites. If you are lucky, the needs coincide in acts of domestic love; if you are not, your man's head turns automatically when a pretty girl passes in the street, or he goes to the porn channels on the computer. He is not to be blamed. Nor does it affect his relationship with you. Love is satisfied, sex isn't quite. He clutches the dummy.

An Unreliable Narrator

Bear in mind, of course, that you must take your instruction from a very flawed person. She wouldn't want to make you anxious by being perfect. Your writer spent last night in the spare room following a domestic row. Voices were raised, someone broke a glass, she broke the washing machine by trying to wrench open the door while it was in the middle of its spin cycle.

Domestic rows do not denote domestic unhappiness. They do suggest a certain volatility in a relationship. Sense might suggest that if the morning wakes to the lonely heaviness that denotes a row the night before, you have no business describing your marriage as 'happy'. But sense and experience also suggest that you have made your own contribution to the way you now feel. And the early sun beats in the windows and it seems an insult to your maker to maintain a grudge when the morning is so glorious.

You hear the sound of the vacuum cleaner downstairs. Soon it will be safe to go down and have a companionable breakfast without even putting on your shoes for fear of slivers of broken glass. Storms pass, the sun shines again. Yes, you are happy.

What the quarrel was about I cannot for the life of me remember.

Except of course now the washing machine doesn't work. When it comes to domestic machinery, retribution comes fast. In other areas of life it may come slowly. But it always does come, in terms of lost happiness, in distance from heaven, in the non-appearance of angels.

And since this book comes to your writer through the luminiferous aether, that notoriously flimsy and deceptive substance, Victorian equivalent of the dark matter of which scientists now claim the universe is composed, what is said is open to interpretation. It is not the Law.

Why, Why?

Like it or not, we are an animal species. Darwinian principles apply. We have evolved into what we are today. We did not spring ready-made into the twenty-first century. The human female is born and bred to select a mate, have babies, nurture them and, having completed this task, die. That is why we adorn ourselves, sweep the cave, attract the best man we can, spite unsuccessful lovers, fall in love and keep a man at our side as long as we can. We are hardwired to do it, for the sake of our children.

Whether a woman wants babies or not, whether she has them or not, is irrelevant. Her physiology and her emotions behave as if she does. Her hormones are all set up to make her behave like a female member of the tribe. The female brain differs from the male even in appearance. Pathologists can tell which is which just by looking,

(Of course if a woman doesn't want to put up with her female destiny she can take testosterone in adult life and feel and be more like a man. Though it is better, I feel, to work with what you have. And that early foetal drenching in oestrogen, when the female foetus decides at around eight weeks that female is the way it's going to stay, is pretty final.)

In her young and fec
call upon science anc
control, in order n
grow older, as nurt
nature, it becomes
less fertile. B: We
marvel is that
pregnancies, not so many.

It's beyond all r
the male impul
the unit can
and create
can get
surprise
The
of

To fall in love is to succumb to ...
Common sense may tell us it's a daft thing to
do. Still we do it. We can't help it, most of us,
once or twice in a lifetime. Oestrogen levels
soar, serotonin plummets. Nature means us to
procreate.

(Odd, the fall in serotonin symptomatic of
falling in love. Serotonin, found in
chocolate, makes us placid and receptive.
A serotonin drop make us anxious, eager,
sexy and on our toes. Without serotonin,
perhaps, we are more effective in
courtship.)

Following the instructions of the blueprint for
courtship, the male of the human species open
doors for us, bring us gifts and forages for us.
If he fails to provide, we get furious, even
when we ourselves are the bigger money
earners. We batter on the doors of the CSA.

...ason. It is also, alas, part of ...se to leave the family as soon as ... survive without him and go off ...nother. (Now that so many women ...y perfectly well without men, the ... is that men stay around at all.)

...tribe exercises restraint upon the excesses ...the individual, however, and so we end up ...ith marriage, divorce laws, sexual-harassment suits and child support. The object of our erotic attention also has to conform to current practices, no matter what instinct says. *'Under 16? Too bad!' 'Your pupil? Bad luck!'* Nature says, *'Kill the robber, the interloper.'* Nurture says, *'No, call the police.'* The sanction, the disapproval of the tribe, is very powerful. Exile is the worst fate of all. Without the protection of the tribe, you die.

Creatures of the Tribe

We do not define ourselves by our animal nature. We are more than creatures of a certain species. We are moral beings. We are ingenious and inquisitive, have intelligence, self-control and spirituality. We understand health and hormones. We develop technology to make our lives easier. We live far longer, thanks to medical science, than nature, left to its own devices, would have us do. We build complicated societies. Many of us choose not have babies, despite our bodies' instinctive craving for them. We socialize men not to desert us; we also, these days, socialize ourselves not to need them.

'I don't dress to attract men,' women will say. *'I dress to please myself.'* But the pleasure women have in the candlelit bath before the party, the arranging and rearranging of the hair, the elbowing of other women at the half-price sale, is instinctive. It's an overflow from courting behaviour. It's also competitive, whether we admit it or not. *'I am going to get the best man. Watch out, keep off!'*

To make friends is instinctive. We stick to our age groups. We cluster with the like-minded. That way lies the survival of the tribe. A woman needs friends to help her deliver the baby, to stand watch when the man's away. But she must also be careful: other women can steal your alpha male and leave you with a beta.

See in shopping, source of such pleasure, also the intimidation of rivals. *'My Prada handbag so outdoes yours—crawl away!'* And she will, snarling.

And if her man's genes seem a better bet than your man's, nab him. Nature has no morality.

Any good feminist would dismiss all this as 'biologism'—the suggestion that women are helpless in the face of their physiology. Of course we are not, but there's no use denying it's at the root of a great deal of our behaviour, and indeed of our miseries. When instincts conflict with each other, when instinct conflicts with socialization, when nature and nurture pull us different ways, that's when the trouble starts.

'I want another éclair.'

Agony.

Well, take the easy way out. Say to yourself, *'One's fine, two's not.'* No one's asking for perfection. And anxiety is inevitable.

A parable.

Once Bitten, Twice Shy

Picture the scene. It's Friday night. David and Letty are round at Henry and Mara's place, as is often the case, sharing a meal. They're all young professionals in their late twenties, good-looking and lively as such people are. They've unfrozen the fish cakes, thawed the block of spinach and cream, and Henry has actually cleaned and boiled organic potatoes. After that it's cheese, biscuits and grapes. Nothing nicer. And Mara has recently bought a proper dinner set so the plates all match.

They all met at college. Now they live near each other. They're not married, they're partnered. But they expect and have so far received fidelity. They have all even made quasi-nuptial contracts with their partner, so should there be a split the property can be justly and fairly assigned. All agree the secret of successful relationships is total honesty.

After graduation Henry and Mara took jobs with the same city firm so as to be together. Mara is turning out to be quite a high-flyer. She earns more than Henry does. That's okay. She's bought herself a little Porsche, buzzes around. That's fine.

'Now I can junk up the Fiesta with auto mags, gum wrappers and Coke tins without Mara interfering,' says Henry.

Letty and David work for the same NHS hospital. She's a radiographer; he is a medical statistician. Letty is likely to stay in her job, or one like it, until retirement, gradually working her way up the promotional ladder, such is her temperament. David is more flamboyant. He's been offered a job at *New Scientist*. He'll probably take it.

Letty would like to get pregnant, but they're having difficulty and Letty thinks perhaps David doesn't really want a baby, which is why it isn't happening.

Letty does have a small secret from David. She consults a psychic, Leah, on Friday afternoons when she leaves work an hour earlier than on other days. She doesn't tell David because she thinks he'd laugh.

'I see you surrounded by babies,' says Leah one day, after a leisurely gaze into her crystal ball.

'Fat chance,' says Letty.

'Is your husband a tall fair man?' asks Leah.

18

'He isn't my husband, he's my partner,' says Letty crossly, 'and actually he's rather short and dark.'

Leah looks puzzled and changes the subject.

But that was a couple of weeks back. This is now. Two bottles of Chilean wine with the dinner, a twist of weed which someone gave Mara for a birthday present . . . and which they're not sure they'll use. They're happy enough as they are. Medical statisticians, in any case, do not favour the use of marijuana.

Henry owns a single e, which someone for reasons unknown gave him when Mara bought the Porsche, saying happiness is e-shaped. He keeps it in his wallet as a kind of curiosity, a challenge to fate.

'You're crazy,' says Letty, when he brings it out to show them. 'Suppose the police stopped you? You could go to prison.'

'I don't think it's illegal to possess a single tablet,' says David. 'Only to sell them.'

He is probably right. Nobody knows for sure. Henry puts it away. It's gone kind of greyish and dusty from too much handling, anyway, and so much observation. Ecstasy is what other people do.

Mara's mobile sings 'Il Toreador'. Mara's mother has been taken ill at home in Cheshire. It sounds as if she might have had a stroke. She's only 58. The ambulance is on its way. Mara, who loves her mother dearly, decides she must drive north to be there for her. No, Mara insists, Henry isn't to come with her. He must stay behind to hold the fort, clear the dinner, make apologies at work on Monday if it's bad and Mara can't get in. 'You'd only be in the way,' she adds. 'You know what men are like in hospitals.' That's how Mara is: decisive. And now she's on her way, thrum, thrum, out of their lives, in the Porsche.

Now there are only Henry, David and Letty to finish the second bottle. David's phone sings 'Ode to Beauty' as the last drop is drained. To open another bottle or not to open another bottle—that's the discussion. Henry opens it, thus solving the problem. It's David's father. There's been a break-in at the family home in Cardiff, the robbers were disturbed and now the police are there. The digital camera has gone and 180 photos of sentimental value and some jewellery and a handbag. David's mother is traumatized and can David make it to Cardiff for the weekend?

'Of course,' says David.

'Can I come?' asks Letty, a little wistfully. She doesn't want to be left alone.

But David says no, it's a long drive, and his parents and the Down's sister will be upset and he'll need to concentrate on them. Better for Letty to stay and finish the wine and Henry will walk her home.

Letty feels more than a little insulted. Doesn't it even occur to David to feel jealous? Is it that he trusts Letty or that he just doesn't care what happens to her? And is he really going to Cardiff or is he just trying to get away from her? Perhaps he has a mistress and that's why he doesn't want to have a baby by her.

David goes and Letty and Henry are left together, both feeling abandoned, both feeling resentful.

Henry and Letty are the ones who love too much. Mara and David love too little. It gives them great power. Those who love least win.

Henry and Letty move out onto the balcony because the evening is so warm and the moon so bright they hardly need a candle to roll the joint. On warm days Mara likes to sit on this balcony to dry her hair. She's lucky. All Mara has to do is dunk her hair in the basin and let it dry naturally and if it falls heavy and silky and smooth. Mara is so lucky in so many respects.

And now Henry walks over to where Letty sits in the moonlight, all white silky skin and bare shoulders and pale-green linen shift which flatters her slightly dull complexion, and slides his hands over her shoulders and down almost to where her breasts start and then takes them away.

'Sorry,' he says. 'I shouldn't have done that.'

'No, you shouldn't,' she says.

'I wanted to,' he said.

'I wanted you to do it too. I think it's the moon. Such a bright night. And see, there's Venus beside her, shining bright.'

'Good Lord!' he says. 'Think of the trouble!'

'But life can get kind of boring,' Letty says. She, the little radiographer, wants her excitements too. Thrum, thrum, thrum goes Mara, off in the Porsche! Why shouldn't it be like that for Letty too? She deserves Henry. Mara doesn't. She'd be nice to him. Letty's skin is still alive to his touch and wanting more.

'But we're not going to, are we?' he says.

'No,' says Letty. 'Mara's my friend.'

'More to the point,' he says, 'David's your partner.'

They think about this for a little while.

'Cardiff and Cheshire,' says Letty. 'Too good to be true. That gives us all night.'

'Where?' asks Henry.

'Here,' says Letty.

All four have in the past had passing fantasies about what it would be like to share a bed and a life with the other—have wondered if, at the student party where they all met, Henry had paired off with Letty, David with Mara, what their lives would have been like. The fantasies have been quickly subdued in the interests of friendship and expediency. But Mara's sheets are more expensive than Letty's, her bed is broader. The City pays more than the NHS. Letty would love to sleep in Mara's bed.

'We could go to your place,' says Henry. To elbow David out of his own bed would be very satisfactory. Henry is stronger and taller than David; Henry takes what he wants when he wants it. Henry has wit and cunning, the kind which enables you to steal another man's woman from under his nose.

But Letty's envy is stronger than Henry's urge to crush his rivals. They agree to stay where they are. They agree this is greater than either of them. They share the e, looking into each other's eyes as if they were toasting one another in some foreign land. It is in fact an aspirin, but since they both believe it's ecstasy, it has the effect of relieving themselves of responsibility for their own actions. Who, drug-crazed, can help what they do?

They tear off each other's clothes. Mara's best and most seductive apricot chiffon nightie is under the pillow. Letty puts it on. Henry makes no objection. It is the one Mara wears, he has come to believe, when she means to refuse him. Too tired, too cross, just not interested. He pushes the delicate fabric up over Letty's thighs with even more satisfaction. He doesn't care if he tears it.

'Shouldn't you be wearing a condom?' she asks.

'I don't like them,' he says.

'Neither do I,' she says.

For ten minutes Letty is supremely happy. The dark, rich places of the flesh unfold and surround her with forgetfulness. She is queen of all places and people. She can have as many men as she wants, just snap her fingers and there they are. She has infinite power. She feels wholly beautiful, consummately desired, part of the breathing, fecund universe, at one with the Masai girl, the Manhattan bride, every flower that ever stooped to mix its pollen, every bird that sings its joy to heaven. And every one of Henry's plunges is a delightful dagger in Mara's heart, his every powerful thrust a reproach to pallid, cautious David.

Then Letty finds herself shifting out of a blissful present into a perplexing future. She's worrying about the sheets. This is condomless sex. What about stains? Will Mara notice? She could launder them— there's a splendid washer-dryer in the utility room, but supposing it broke down mid-wash? Henry could possibly argue that he spilt wine on the sheets—as indeed he has, and honey too, now she comes to think of it. She is very sticky. Can Mara's chiffon nightie be put in the machine or must it be hand washed?

'Is something the matter?' he asks.

'No,' she says.

But she no longer feels safe. Supposing Mara gets a call from her family on the way to Cheshire and turns back? Supposing she and Henry are discovered? Why is she doing this? Is she mad?

Her body shudders in spite of herself. She rather resents it. An orgasm crept up on her when she was trying to concentrate on important things. She decides sex is just mechanical. She'd rather have David, anyway. His penis is less effective and smaller than Henry's, but it's familiar and feels right. David must never find out about this. Perhaps she doesn't want a baby as much as she thought she did. In any case she can't have a baby that isn't David's. What if she got pregnant now? She'd have to have an abortion, and it's against her principles, and it would have to be secret because fathers can now claim rights to unborn embryos.

Henry rolls off her. Letty makes languid disappointment noises but she's rather relieved. He is heavier than David.

Henry's phone goes. He answers it. Mara is

stuck behind an accident on the M6 north of Manchester,

'Yes,' says Henry, 'I walked Letty home.'

Now Letty's cross because Henry has denied her. Secrecy seems sordid. And she hates liars. And Mara? What about Mara? Mara is her friend. They've studied together, wept together, bought clothes together and supported each other through bad times, good times. Mara and her Porsche and her new wardrobe have all seemed a bit much, true, but she sees why Mara puts Henry down from time to time. He's not only irritating but untrustworthy. How could you trust your life to such a man? She ought to warn Mara about that, but how can she? Poor Mara, stuck behind an ambulance in the early hours in the far north while her partner betrays her with her best friend . . .

Henry is licking honey off his fingertips suggestively. 'Shall we do that again?' he asks. 'Light of my life.'

'No,' says Letty and rolls out of bed. Her bare sticky feet touch the carpet and she is saved.

Moral

Few of us can resist temptation the
first time round, and we should not
blame ourselves too much if we fail.
It's the second time that counts. Let
sin pass lightly on and over. Persist
in it and it wears your soul away.

Letty's sense of guilt evaporates, washed
away in the knowledge of her own virtue and
fondness for her friend. Guilt is to the soul as
pain is to the body. It is there to keep us away
from danger, from extinction.

And good Lord, think what might have
happened had Letty stayed for a second
round! As it was she got into her own bed
just minutes before David came through the
door. His father had rung from Cardiff and the
jewellery had been found and the burglary
hadn't happened after all. Letty hadn't had a
bath, thinking she'd leave that until the
morning, but David didn't seem to notice.
Indeed, he fell on her with unusual ardour
and the condom broke and he didn't even
seem to mind.

If she'd stayed in Mara's bed David would
have come round to find Letty and at worst

killed Henry—fat chance!—and at best told Mara, or if not that then he'd have been able to blackmail Letty for the rest of her life. *'Do this or I'll tell Mara'*—and she'd have had to do it, whatever it was: go whoring, get a further degree (not that there wasn't some attraction in surrendering autonomy . . .)

But as it was it all worked out okay. Letty had her 10 minutes of sublime pleasure, felt anxious, felt guilty, and was rewarded by having her cake and eating it too. I don't know what happened to the sheets. I daresay Henry calmed down enough to put them through the washer-dryer and get them on the bed again before Mara got back. I hope he had the sense to rinse out her nightie in the basin at hand temperature, not hot.

I do know that in the following week Henry sold the Fiesta and got a Jaguar which could outrun the Porsche any day, and he used the joint account to do it. He felt better about himself.

I allow Letty, having observed the moon, to sleep illicitly with Henry once, but not twice. It is a balancing act and she got it right.

It is doing what you should, if only in the end, and not what you want which makes others respect and like you, and to be respected and liked by others is a very good way to be happy.

Save your moral strength for what is important.

The Inevitability of Anxiety

What makes women happy? Nothing, not for more than ten minutes at a time. Anxiety, doubt and guilt break through.

'Supposing my boyfriend comes back?' 'Have I left the fish out for the cat?' 'Should I be doing this?'

Blame nature.

It's the hormones doing it, interfering with our happiness, not the mysterious thing called *me*.

Instinct rewards us by gratifying our sensual appetites. It also punishes us if we go too far.

It is when we are following the promptings of instinct, doing what nature suggests, going through the motions of procreation—however unlikely they are to succeed—even in the midst of our triumph and greatest pleasure that other warring instincts set in. *'Clean the cave, keep the baby safe, are the food stores okay? What's that rustling at the back of the cave? Can it be the sabre-tooth tiger? We can't just lie here enjoying ourselves! Hasn't he finished yet? Is the fire going out? Might a vulture swoop down to get the baby? What's the*

31

woman in the next cave up to? Has he noticed my spare tyre? Is she a better bet than me? Will he go to her?'

While he, the man, is thinking solely about pleasure and completion, concentrating on the task in hand, our female minds are already wandering.

He: 'Is something the matter, darling? You seem to have lost interest.'

She: 'I just remembered I left the butter out of the fridge. Sorry. Now where were we?'

Our instincts overlap and contradict each other: the one to make babies struggles with the need to look after the ones already there; the one to compete with our friends with our need to have them at our side. It leaves us confused.

Sex with the new true love brings bliss, optimism, unguarded delight—and then: *'Am I too fat, will he notice my varicose vein, will the baby wake, will his wife come back, should I have told him I loved him?'*

With the wedding, it's all *'Will the flowers arrive, should I have worn this tatty veil, should I really be doing this?'*

With the promotion, *'Will my friends hate me, will my new office be okay, will my partner leave me if I earn more than him?'*

The pleasure in the new baby is balanced out by the anxiety that goes with bonding. Bonding is one of the worst tricks instinct plays on us. The baby cries; the mother leaps to attention. It is a lifetime's sentence to anxiety. It doesn't get better with time. And it is not open to reason. Experience may tell us that the teenager late home is usually late home. But mother love is panicking: *'He's come off his bike. There'll be a call from the hospital.'*

The baby's quiet—and it makes you happy and proud to have got him through to the end of the day. *'But perhaps he's stopped breathing?'* Wake him and see!

There are so many things to be anxious about. The baby's not breathing. You only mascaraed one eye this morning. Sheer pleasure can trigger anxiety. When you're nibbling caviare, or taking a taxi home loaded, or feeling spaced out at a concert, what do you think? *'I shouldn't be here. I am going to be punished. I shouldn't be doing this. Something terrible is about to happen. I do not deserve to be happy.'*

Well, maybe you don't. That may be the trouble.

We are more than creatures of the cave, ruled by instinct. We are moral beings as well.

Guilt, Offshoot of Anxiety

Guilt also stands between you and enjoyment. It's an offshoot of anxiety.

'Shouldn't have done this, shouldn't have done that. Shouldn't have had a one-night stand. Shouldn't have eaten a bar of chocolate . . .'

It too is instinctive, hardwired in. It applies itself to any number of situations. When we succumb to 'inappropriate' sexual desire, eat the forbidden chocolate—anything that makes us feel bad—that's when the instinctive self, determined to satisfy its appetites, is in conflict with the socialized self.

'Ought not to endanger my relationship. Ought to lose weight.'

Feel it in its purest form when you neglect your children: *'Three in the morning, the baby's crying, but I'm too tired to bother.'* Baby wins: eventually you stir yourself, get out of bed and see to it. Thus Mother Nature, that unseeing, unthinking, callous creature, ensures the continuation of the race.

Whether or not you have children, the capacity to feel guilt is there. Stronger in some than in others. Certainly stronger in women than in men.

She: 'We need to get back, darling. The babysitter's waiting up.'

He: 'Oh, for heaven's sake. What do we pay her for?'

Guilt is society's safeguard. If you don't feel guilt at all they declare you're a psychopath and lock you up, and quite right too.

Let me add to that—just to counter the effect of so much Darwinian reductionism, which is true enough but there are other truths as well, namely that we have a spiritual life—that guilt is the soul's safeguard. And if the soul is safeguarded, we start from a higher level of life content than we would otherwise do. If you are good—abstain from bitchiness, doing others down, malice and complaint—people like you. If you are liked, you tend to have a good life.

Be good and you'll be happy. Be happy and you'll be good and go to heaven.

As a corollary, if you don't respond to the promptings of guilt, you might very well go to hell—in other words, fall into a depression, get ill and end up with no friends.

The Value of Guilt

You could see the 'oughts' and 'shoulds' which litter our lives as a nuisance, as contrary to our own self-interest. So our partner suffers because we were unfaithful, so our mother is lonely and upset because we didn't visit, so our children weep uncomforted. So who cares? *'I really deserve a holiday. I deserve it because I'm me.'* Stuff and nonsense.

'Now at last,' says the new-style granny, abstaining from babysitting, spending the children's inheritance, *'I'm going to do something for* myself.*'*

You won't enjoy it, you know. You will feel guilty and selfish every minute of your sun-soaked, pampered holiday, and so you should.

Therapists may well try and iron the emotion of guilt out of us, and some do, seeing it as 'negative'. By which they mean it's uncomfortable, painful and inconvenient, and aren't we trying to achieve happiness here? *'Look to your own skin,'* they advise. *'Do*

36

what you want.'

Alexander Crowley, black magician, rapist and philosopher of Edwardian times, self-styled Beast no. 666, had this as his philosophy: *Do what thou wilt shall be the whole of the Law.* It was an attitude seen as very shocking at the time, even satanic. If it doesn't sound all that unreasonable now it may be our loss as, seeking validation for our bad actions, we virtuously pursue the 'authenticity of our feelings' (*'I have to leave you and the kids because I'm in love'*) and decide we deserve every good thing, in the words of the shampoo ad, *because we're worth it.*

Self-esteem can go too far—a little low self-esteem might not come amiss as we consider our faults and failures. On our deathbeds the memory of the authenticity of our feelings might not seem as important as the love and company of our friends and relatives.

There is a truly simple answer to the pains of guilt: *If you feel bad about it, don't do it.*

Now there's an old-fashioned doctrine. Step by step, little by little, do what you *should*, not what you *want.*

Conscience is to the soul as pain is to the body. It keeps you out of harm's way.

Doing Bad and Feeling Worse

There are little everyday acts of meanness, little evils which are under our control, little tactlessnesses meant to hurt, which contribute to our own unhappiness. For hidden somewhere within us is the fear of retaliation. *'If I do this, you might do that.'* You get wary and untrusting. Meanness shows—it's bad for the complexion, gives you a dull skin, wrinkles and squinty eyes. You end up, in fact, with the face you deserve.

And then there are the great big destructive acts, like bringing your family toppling down like a house of cards. It's quite easy to do and you will always find allies.

Daughter: 'You were a terrible mother. That's why I'm such a mess. My therapist says so. I hate you. I'm not letting you see your grandchildren any more—you're such a monster you might do the same to them as you did to me.'

Mother: 'But I did the best I could. You are the meaning of my life. I love you the way you love your own children.'

Daughter: 'Daddy, you must have abused me when I was a little girl. My therapist says there's no other explanation for my feelings of hostility and depression.'

Father: 'Perhaps you were just born that way. Perhaps you should go to church and not a therapist. Meanwhile, thanks a million for breaking up the family. I'm off.'

One day you come to your senses and wonder what it was all about, and you can remember everything, but there's no one to tell, no family shoulders left to cry on, and your own children don't seem to seek your company.

Conclusion

There are some truly bad therapists out there as well as some very good ones.

Proud, Defiant and Unhappy

You can take the proud and defiant path through life, of course. Some do and get away with it. You can decide you have problems because you let yourself be trampled on and go to assertiveness classes.

It has never seemed to me, however, that assertiveness classes have done anyone any good. My friend Valerie went to one, complaining that other people walked all over her. My own feeling was that she was the one who normally did the trampling, while worrying about her self-esteem and tendency to self-effacement. When she returned after her two-week course she bullied more, smiled less and her self-esteem was sky-high. It's true she got a rise, but she lost her boyfriend. Justice was on her side, but life wasn't.

The fewer the mini-nastinesses we do—and we all do them—the better able we will be to deal with the real, great, imponderable areas of unhappiness when they come along. Which they do, unasked, in everyone's life.

Moral

If you haven't anything nice to say,
don't say anything at all. Smile
though you want to spit. When in
doubt, do nothing.

This flies in the face of contemporary wisdom, I know. Valerie was told to give voice to her anger (*or she'd get cancer*), speak emotional truths (*it was only fair to herself*), claim the authenticity of her feelings (*'I feel, therefore I'm right'*) never fake orgasm (*it's a lie, an indignity*) and in general claim her rights and seek justice in the home and at work. Above all she must never be persuaded into making the office coffee, because she was worth more than that.

40

Valerie sounded off at her boss when he said it would be nice to have a cup of coffee, and he said that was the last straw, he was tired of being bullied, and he fired her. She told her mother she'd rather she didn't phone the office because of her Birmingham accent and her mother spent her savings—those that hadn't gone on Valerie's expensive education—on a little cottage in France and wouldn't be there to babysit when she was needed—not that there was much question of babies any more, since Valerie was 41 and her boyfriend got so nervous in the end about not 'giving' her an orgasm (which didn't seem in his power to give anyway) that the sex dried up altogether and he left. And she had to make her own coffee in her lonely home, while trying to find a lawyer willing to accept her unfair dismissal case, and these days caffeine gave her palpitations, and her mother was out of even mobile range.

An Alternative Therapy: Prayer

Suffer a pang of remorse when in bed with your best friend's boyfriend and act upon it by getting out of the bed, and you will have less sensual pleasure in the short term, but it is amazing how gratifying doing the right thing is. Your best friend may not see it quite like that, of course, concentrating only on the fact that you were in the bed in the first place.

But pray God she will never find out.

I mean that. Actually pray. Gather a few forces around you. The way to be happy, to forestall anxiety and guilt, is to be good.

The world being what it is, you may not know what praying is. (Look it up on the Internet and you can't find a definition.) But this is how it goes. You sit down. You create a mental space around you. Shutting your eyes helps. Hands steepled together helps: you're enclosing yourself within yourself, making a separation between yourself and what's outside you. Which, you will find, if you develop the antennae, is a kind of breathing presence, the majesty of existence itself. You are part of it.

Pray for others, not yourself. (Praying for yourself is vulgar.) Hold your friends in your mind, household by household. Direct your thoughts towards them, wish them well, enfold them and surround them with goodwill. Family too, of course, but anxieties and practicalities are more likely to break through here. Attention wanders.

You can link what you're doing with a known religion, the Father (*'Dear Holy Father'*), the

Son (*'Dear Lord Jesus'*) or Holy Ghost (though very few pray to him because he is so hard to envisage), or any of the saints (*'Dear St Anthony, help me find my lost sentence'*), or Pan, I suppose, if you're a pantheist (*'Dear Lord Pan, help me find my lost virility'*), or Mother Mary (*'Help me get pregnant'*), but with all these what you are doing is using an intermediary to connect you.

Prayer is easier than meditation, which encourages self-centredness and too great a sense of *'Look at me, meditating!'* You seldom fall asleep when praying for others, as you do when meditating. You just stop when concentration fails.

Perfection is impossible to achieve, of course. But we can try, and angels will attend us, and we can take pleasure from the gentle air of their beating wings.

A Joke: Man Prays to God

'Dear God, let me win the lottery!' The voice is piercing, shrill and desperate, amongst all the others pleading to God for help. It goes on for week after week, Wednesday after Saturday after Wednesday: *'Let me win the lottery!'*

The Almighty does his best to ignore the voice, but finally he can't stand it any more. He speaks like thunder from the clouds. *'Okay,'* says God, *'tell you what, I'll meet you halfway. Buy a ticket.'*

The Major Enemies of Happiness

Forget guilt, forget anxiety. There are real enemies of happiness out there, real tribulations, which are powerful and not self-inflicted. Things that just happen.

Difficulties Along the Way

Old age

Illness

Bereavement

Isolation

Debt

Bitterness

Old Age

Make no mistake about it, money helps. It makes most troubles easier, while not necessarily solving problems.

Failing money, friends help—as does a long record of good behaviour and kindness to others. The comfort of strangers, if sought, is often there. What you put into life at the beginning you can take out with dividends at the end.

Old age seen from the outside can look horrific. But if you're in there in that derelict body it's still you; there are still pleasures and ambitions left to you. You are Ivan in the Russian story by Solzhenitsyn, the man in the prison camp who guarded his piece of dry bread successfully all day, and when he finally ate it, enjoyed incomparable pleasure. Seen from the outside, it was dreadful; from the inside, triumphant. May it be like that for you.

Illness

Illness is bad. But it can be very interesting, especially if it's your own. Symptoms are fascinating. It's another world, a bubble one, perhaps, and precarious, but those in it have already found a way to live with it. The skill of physicians and surgeons is inspiring. As is other people's selflessness. The walls of your experience may narrow to the width of a hospital bed, but it is still a stage, this is your drama and you are the centre of it. A good performance will get good reviews. Understand and please your audience: the visitors who may or may not cluster round your bed; at the very least the volunteer who brings round the library books or the man who wheels the trolley of newspapers and junk food.

'How are you today?' they ask. Well, tell them. That's pleasure in itself. If ill enough, you are excused selflessness and martyrdom.

And if you are temporarily in a hospital ward, try not to hate it. Go with the flow. The social life of the ward is rich and strange, never mind the routine. People elaborate their symptoms and treatments with a relish others share. They support and understand each other. They joke about death. The ward is a mini-tribe, sharing experiences.

In the private ward you have your comfort but you can be lonely, and another patient is more likely to come to your aid than a nurse. Sometimes money is not the universal solution.

When Children Are Ill

There is nothing good to be said about the serious illness of a child and not much comfort to be offered to the parents involved, other than to try to shift the perspective, see the

46

small body as too frail and weak to support the intense existence of the mind and soul of this particular child. See how the latter exists, how clearly and powerfully it becomes apparent even as the body fails. The inner being makes itself clear—let the parents try to gain strength from it. Difficult, because parental distress is based in one of the most powerful instincts we have: to protect and save the children. The mind has little defence in these circumstances. The soul has. It is strong in the child. Those who suffer with children will understand the concept.

You can pray, though your sense of a benign universe will be somewhat blunted. That in itself is unsettling. The prayers would have to overcome your sense that you are picked out by fate for cruel and unjust punishment.

And it might help you, selflessly, to let the child go, to not struggle pointlessly for the continuation of its existence.

You could try Lourdes. I haven't been there, but they do say that a community of the like-minded, on the edges of despair, within which you don't have to explain yourself, with standards you can adapt to, however idiosyncratic and peculiar they may seem to the healthy and flourishing rationalist you once were lucky enough to be, can be a great comfort. You're with the tribe you have inherited. It might seem grotty compared to the one you were born into, but it is a tribe.

Bereavement and Isolation
We'll get on to these universal enemies later, and in more detail, when we are feeling stronger. I can be quite cheerful about bereavement, there are cures for isolation, and as for debt, well . . .

Debt
It's probably your own fault. You had a vision of yourself which did not accord with reality. You upgraded yourself to a wealthier sort of person than you actually were. It happens. You should have listened to the Voice of Guilt. You have my every sympathy. Earn your way out of it.

Bitterness
Very little in life is fair. Some of us are born with longer legs than others. Some of us are born into poverty in the Sahara desert, others into prosperity in leafy suburbs.

It's unfair that some are born thin, active, nervy ectomorphs and others are born rounded, easy-going endomorphs. Society these days smiles on the former rather than the latter, who have to spend their lives on diets, never eating what they want, except in those few places left in the world where obesity is valued.

Seeking natural justice is absurd: justice does not exist in nature. Seeking justice in the home is okay, but tends to end in exhaustion: it can be easier to wash his socks than argue that he should do it.

Resenting men, an emotion familiar to most women, is understandable but pointless. Don't let it make you bitter. Some things are just not fair. It is not fair that for men the culmination of sex is always an orgasm—or at least for 98 per cent of them—and for women it is not.

Sex

Sources of Envy

10 per cent of women never experience orgasm.

20 per cent occasionally do.

50 per cent sometimes do.

20 per cent usually do.

10 per cent always do.

Or so the current figures say. But figures change. Someone in the 10 per cent 'always' category suddenly goes down to the next division: *'My partner came back from his trip and he'd grown a beard.'* Someone in the 'never' group claims now to be in the 'sometimes' category: *'I met another man.'* But the broad pattern is clear. The pleasure so liberally bestowed upon men by nature is only grudgingly given to women.

Of course women resent it. Listen to any conversation between women when men aren't there: at the hen night, on the factory floor, over the garden fence, at the English Lit.

tutorial. Women may laugh and joke, but actually they're furious. *'They can, we can't, unfair, unfair.'* They may not know what's biting them, but that's it.

But facts are facts and there we are. Deal with it. Life is not fair. Resenting the fact is no recipe for happiness.

Indeed, the less you think about orgasms the better, since the greatest bar to having one, if we're to believe the research, is wanting one. Best if they creep up on you unawares. Women are at their most orgasmic when they are least anxious, but wondering why you're not having one can make you very anxious indeed. Which is ironic, since what you want most you're going to get least.

But a lot of life is like that. Want too much and it's snatched away. An attitude of careless insouciance is more likely to pay dividends.

Because really, having an orgasm or not doesn't matter in the great scheme of things, just as having an éclair or not doesn't matter. Life goes on pretty much the same with or without. There are other pleasures. There's true love, trust and sensual pleasure. Or, if you're that kind of person, and I hope you are not, the victory of disdain. *'See, knew you were no good in bed.'*

But actually, it's as likely, if not more likely, to be your doing, not his.

Unfair—but what you are after is happiness. Sexual repletion is not a necessary ingredient. Sexual satisfaction can happen anyway, and is not dependent on orgasm. If women were not so often described as 'achieving orgasm' then there would be no sense of failure when they didn't. The word is wrong, not the thing itself.

'I don't do *orgasm'* might be a more useful way of describing yourself, initially, to a partner, and it's a bonus to both if it turns out not to be true. But having an orgasm is not a sign of true love any more than the lack of it is the opposite. I have read letters from girls who think they must end a relationship because sex between them and their true love does not conclude with an orgasm for her. Imagining sex has failed, they feel the relationship has failed. It hasn't—all that has happened has been that she *didn't have an orgasm.* So what? Better, more conducive to happiness, just to see orgasm as an additional extra, something special that happens, a bonus, a surprising gift from heaven which descends like manna from time to time, not your natural-born right— and then a whole raft of unhappiness will be wiped from your life.

In Any Case
Female orgasm has no apparent usefulness to the human race. This puzzles those who think that everything in nature has to have a purpose, those who personalize evolution as if it knew what it was doing and had some end of perfection in sight. Some say muscular spasms help the sperm on its way to the egg; others doubt it. It is not the longing for orgasm which makes the virgin girl fall in love—though it may be the boy's. Another inequality, another injustice!

The peacock's tail demonstrates sexual attraction in overdose as he struts before the female; his voice would be enough to put anyone off. I don't suppose nature was after fairness, trying to balance things in the scales of justice, when she gave with one hand and took away with the other.

Why different birds have different voices no one knows—and no one's worked out what they're *for*—but those with (to our ears) the sweetest voices are the ones who sing the loudest and seem to relish their singing most. I like to think that the thrushes in my garden sing because it occurs to them that it's a beautiful morning and they feel like acknowledging it. It's an irrational thought, but it makes me happy for at least ten minutes, wandering in the garden and listening, but then the sun gets too hot and I worry because I haven't got a hat.

Some say that, like male nipples and the appendix, female orgasm is a mistake which nature has failed to recognize as a non-necessity. Better to see it as a celebration and a reward just for being alive. But there are others—the exhilaration of ideas, conversations, the company of good friends and so on—which probably add up to more.

The Joy of the Fake Orgasm

Just fake. Happy, generous-minded women, not too hung up about emotional honesty, fake. Research tells us that when you do there is *'activity in the part of the motor cortex that relates to the genitals, the amygdala, but not the deactivation of the cerebral cortex that occurs prior and after a genuine orgasm'*. In other words you have to be happy to have an orgasm, but if you have an orgasm you will be happy.

Activate the positive. Deactivate the negative. That's what it's all about.

The more highly educated you are, the more likely you are to fake orgasm. I am not sure what we deduce from that. Is too much intellectual stimulation bad for the love life?

54

Or does it just occur to clever women pretty soon that it's only sensible to fake it?

Genuine orgasm experienced, acknowledged and stored away as one of the uncompromisingly good things in life, you will then no doubt leap out of bed and make breakfast, or squeeze orange juice or pour champagne or whatever your lifestyle, with the words *You are so clever*, or however you express enthusiasm, ringing in his—or her, of course, should you be a lesbian—ears.

If you are sensible you will do exactly the same if you've faked it, because half the pleasure of sex is being nice to the other person, and half is better than none, on the half-full, half-empty cup principle. Clever, judgemental, honourable people who feel deception is unworthy of them, who say, *'But relationships must be based upon truth,'* are likely to be of the half-empty sort.

Remember you are not in pursuit of justice, you are seeking what makes women happy. You must catch it as it flies, and if it flies just out of reach, well, it was a nice sight while it lasted, wasn't it?

Faking is kind to male partners of the new man kind, who like to think they have done their duty by you. Otherwise they too may become anxious and so less able to perform. The more the woman rates 'performance', the more likely the man is to wilt and fail. Do yourself and him a favour, sister: fake it. Then, who knows, as a reward for your kindness, sublime pleasure may creep up on you unawares.

There is a great confusion here between the pleasures of love and the pleasures of sex. Both can carry on along parallel tracks, never touching, to the end of time. Or one day, who's to say, they may meet.

My friend Olivia, now 69, had an orgasm for the first time when she was 54 and nine years into her second marriage. It took her by surprise. But she said it was like learning to ride a bicycle: once you knew how to do it, you could do it all the time. She's been clocking them up ever since. Life does not begin at 20. She was doing well enough without them, was earning a salary at that time as CEO of a media communications firm and had seemed to me to be living a full, even over-full, love life since I first met her when she was 18.

Her first marriage ended in scandal and divorce—her husband, a writer, naming seven co-respondents. (In those days of guilty and innocent, sexual infidelity had to be proved. Illicit couples had to be discovered *in flagrante*, stained sheets produced and so on, before the judge would grant a divorce.) The press went to town. Oddly enough, the naming and shaming did Olivia no harm in the business world. Even then, everyone liked anyone who had their name in the papers. And then the sixties were upon us and a great deal of random sexual activity went on as a matter of course, and after that divorce was not a matter of right or wrong but about the division of property. Meanwhile Olivia rose rocket-like through the corporate world and who is to say, if she had had more orgasms, she would have bothered to reach such heights? A touch of discontent in the night may be good for all of us. Sexual satisfaction, sensual repletion and the irrational sense of gratitude which tends to go with them, may be the last thing a career woman needs.

Most women, I suspect, are after true love, rather than orgasm, though they will put up with many stages on the way, from pure lust to pride assuaged to boredom endured. And even if true love is not on your agenda, it is always gratifying to stir it in others. If faking it helps, do it.

The Naturalness of the Hen Night

Girls together is good, girls together is fun and usually noisy. But notice how bitterness against men seems to be hardwired, as if nature had bred us to be suspicious of the male, on the lookout for bad behaviour. There's something in us of the female cat, not letting the tom near the kittens in case he eats them. Put us together and there's no stopping us. Listen in to the talk and laughter at a girls' night out: anecdotes about the follies of men, jokes about the minimal size of their parts, tales of male vanity and self-delusion—their stumbling mumbleness, their crazy driving.

We egg each other on to disloyalty. We are the women; we close ranks in opposition to men. The food gets cold on the plate in our excitement. The wine is quickly drunk, and more wine, and vodka shorts. We are the Maenads just before Orpheus comes on the scene to get torn to bits.

And then the mirth gets bitter. It isn't really funny, it's real. Someone begins to cry.

Men who leave, men who won't leave, men who fail to provide, men who don't love you after all, men who are a sexual disappointment. Past husbands, vanished partners, the ones who never washed, the ones who had the *au-pair* girl. Men: ridiculous, pathetic, sad.

The noise diminishes and fades away. Silence falls. Time to count heads and divide the bill. Those who have partners slip away, feeling guilty and grateful. Those who haven't go home on their own, or walk each other to the bus, and tell themselves all they need is their friends.

I have in my time enjoyed such gatherings immensely. They are a great pleasure. Life is good. The trick is to pay and leave just before the silence falls. And try not to be the one collecting the money and tipping the waiter.

Go to Norway and Sweden and notice how the restaurants are full of men. Few women eat out. Yet in theory these are super-equal societies. The women, one supposes, can only prefer to stay at home. These all-male meals— tables for four, six, eight, ten, more—tend to be silent, grim affairs. Men like to sit side by side, silently, metaphorically locking horns, and don't seem to have nearly such a good time as women do. But they do seem to get happier as the evening progresses, not the other way round. Life gets better, not worse. It isn't fair.

59

Nothing's fair.

It's unfair that some people like sex a lot, some very little, some not at all. The capacity for pleasure is not doled out equally or fairly.

(It is probably a good idea that people with equivalent levels of sexual energy partner one another, if they want the union to last. People need to wear each other out in bed. Three times a day, three times a week (the norm) or once a year—so long as both are suited, what's the worry?)

Mind you, the easy-orgasmers, the lucky 20 per cent, are not always popular with others. The papers this morning were in a state of outrage about Sandy, a feckless girl of 19 who went on holiday to Spain leaving her three children in the care of a 15-year-old. When summonsed home by the police and the media, she refused to go. She was having too good a time, she said. She had her photo taken burying her head into the bare chest of a semi-naked waiter. I bet she had orgasms at the drop of a hat. She knew how to enjoy herself. She was not anxious. She did not feel guilt. She well and truly broke the ten-minute rule. She stretched it to a whole week of drink, drugs, sex and ecstasy before guilt set in and she flew home. That's one way of doing it.

60

It Isn't Fair But It's a Fact

The fight for gender equality is bad for the looks. It makes no one happy, unless you find some reward in struggling for a justice that evolution failed to deliver. It will just develop your jaw, wrinkle your brow beyond the capacity of Botox to unravel, muddy your complexion so much that no amount of Beauty Flash will clear it, and in general do you no good.

Fight for political justice by all means—join the party, reform and re-educate. Fight for domestic justice—*'Your turn to clean the loo'*—if you must, though personally I don't recommend too much of it, it's too exhausting. But do not fight for physiological equality because it does not exist.

If you have a period pain, you have one. Accept it. Don't fight it. Sit down. Take a pill. A male voice raised is impressive; a female voice raised creates antipathy. Accept it. You are not trying to be a man. You are proud to be a woman. Do not shout your enemies down at the client meeting—leave that to the men. Get your way by smiling sweetly. The end is more important than the means.

Accept that for women happiness comes in short bursts and the ten-minute rule applies.

61

For men it can last as long as a football match before they realize they're late picking up the child from school.

So is the sum of human happiness greater for a man than for a woman? I suspect so. Lucky old them.

Be generous. You can afford to be. At least you occupy the moral high ground, and they know it.

Occupying the Moral High Ground

It's quite nice up here these days. Women can look out over the urban landscape and know they are nicer than men, more co-operative, more empathic, better at communication, better at getting to university and better at getting jobs. Women multi-task—everyone knows. They can do many things at once. Men tend to do one thing at a time. If a woman loses a sock she finds another which will do just as well; a man continues the search until he has found it (albeit in the bin where he threw it), by which time the train has gone and the meeting has begun.

Women abjure the idle languorousness of sexual contentment and get on with things. Women leap out of bed after sex to feed the cat and wash out their smalls so that they'll be dry by morning. Men just go to sleep gratified and satisfied, happy that all is well. (Though if it's not his own bed he may well want to regain it before falling asleep. *I'll call you in the morning,*' he says. Oh yes!)

Women worry in advance. They search through their bags for the dry-cleaning ticket before they even get into the shop. Men wait until they're in there and then hold everyone up.

Just Accept It
Accept gender differences, don't deny them. That way you make the most of what happiness nature did allow you as a woman.

Evolution has allowed you an intellect that's pretty much the same as the male's.

(Though the male bell curve when it comes to IQ is a little more flattened than for the female. That is to say there are more males at the extreme ends of the spectrum—extreme intelligence, extreme lack of it—which is why you get more male double-firsts at Oxford than female and more males held in police cells overnight than females.)

Evolution has also allowed you an aesthetic appreciation equal to that of the male. There are as many men as women listening to flute concertos at the Wigmore Hall, as many men as women wandering round art galleries.

(Nature might slightly favour the male when it comes to creative activity—men's books may be 'better', if less readable, than women's, their paintings fetch more in the art market, and so on—but that claim would take a whole book on its own to discuss.)

The traditionally female qualities of caring and nurturing, sharing and co-operating were not always seen as admirable. Inside the home a woman did them for free; outside the home they commanded low wages. Society favoured to male virtues: dismissing and disposing, self-control and a stiff upper lip. But then women, released by technological advance from the domestic drudgery required just to keep the children alive, have used their new power brilliantly. Theirs are the qualities now most valued in Western society. Forget the old male values of never apologizing, never explaining— they're out-moded. Presidents weep, prime ministers apologize, monarchs explain.

To have to accept your genetic make-up, the femaleness of your body, its irritating habit of keeping menstrual time with the moon, is not so bad a fate. These cosmic forces are too great for you to take on single-handed anyway.

It isn't fair, but it's a fact.

If It Takes a Man to Make You Happy . . .

It's a dreadful assumption to make that just because a woman is a woman she must need a man. I know many a female who's lived happily ever after without one. They may well have a blip in their mid-forties when it occurs to them that being single looks like being a permanent state. That pang of doubt is nature's last-ditch stand against the nurture that persuades a woman that a man is an optional extra. But the automatic, instinctive pairings-off of the under-thirties are a long way behind her now. Crowded rooms are not for looking across in case she sees the man of her dreams, but for meeting friends, elegant conversation and making useful business contacts. She is the contented singleton. She tried sex and found it wanting. She never met a man she liked or respected enough to join forces with on a permanent basis. She has money enough to enjoy her life.

My mother, coming from a generation in which any man was better than none, would have described her as 'too picky'. And today's educated young woman is certainly in something of a pickle, what with both nature (her traditional selectivity when it comes to choosing a mate) and nurture (our current understanding that compared to women men are crude, loud-voiced, doltish creatures; look at any TV ad to see it) persuading her that nothing but a truly alpha male will do for her. That knight in shining armour crashing through the undergrowth to find her has to be better born than she is, better educated and richer—women have such a passion for marrying their superiors—and it gets harder and harder to find such a man.

And the girls of the tribe, the ones in her age group, will be watching and vetting to make sure she gets it right.

'You can do better than that,' they'll say. (That's tribe-talk too. Friends as arbiters of sexual choice is a timeless scenario.) Their judgement these days isn't so good, that's the trouble. It's self-conscious, and probably self-interested too. They need someone to sit next to in the cinema, to laugh and giggle with. The pleasures of a night out with friends outweigh the pleasures of a date. Men just look at films and grunt; girls *talk*.

But anyway, here she is, and life is good, and what should she want with a man? If she needs to change a tyre she can use her mobile and call a garage. Once she had to stand by the side of the road showing a leg. (She could do it herself, but whoever wanted to do that? My dear, the oil, the spanners, the weakness of the unaccustomed wrist!) The pang soon fades. She is happy again, and good for her.

But if you still believe that only with a man can you be truly happy, then you had better find one.

Finding a Man
There are two ways of doing it:

1. *He chases and you run.* This requires nerve, and you to be higher on the scale of partner-desirability than he. If you are convinced that you are—your beauty outweighing his wealth, for example—then give it a go. Female disdain is attractive, but you have to have looks to get away with it. Your handbook will be *The Rules.*

2. *You sit quiet and smile.* Never when in the company of the man you're after do you give him a hard time. You never argue, quarrel, demand your rights, reproach him, give him one iota of emotional,

intellectual or physical discomfort. This is the best ploy for the 80 per cent of women who were not born with symmetrical features and a sexy body, who have wiry hair and a muddy complexion and cannot be bothered to have cosmetic surgery. Your handbook will be *The Surrendered Wife*.

A man, research tells us, plays the sexual field until he decides he's ready to settle down. Then he looks round the field of his female acquaintance and picks the one he likes the most. Let it be you. If that's what you want.

A woman, research tells us, goes searching for the perfect mate within her field of expectation (the rich marry the rich, remember, the beautiful the beautiful) and may go on searching too long. Her vision of herself can be inflated (*'Because I'm worth it!'*), her standards higher than is practical. That is why we have so many talented, beautiful, high-earning, intelligent, single young women about, while their male compatriots are safely tucked away in the suburbs, shacked up with some dim and dozy wife. Too picky!

Category 2 women fail when they behave as if they were in category 1. Only in romantic novels does Mr Darcy marry Elizabeth Bennett. He ran, she ran faster, he turned round and caught her. In real life he might have set her up as his mistress in Maida Vale, but marriage? No. On the scale of partner-desirability they did not match.

Let me tell you the parable of a woman who feared that she lived a dim and dozy life but found great happiness because she was good.

Happy Yuletide, Schiphol

And we'd been so clever. We would catch the 15.40 from Schiphol Airport on the 24th and be back in Bristol by 17.55 to pick up the hire car and be in Okehampton in good time for Christmas Eve dinner with goose, mashed potatoes, red cabbage and a fine Rhone wine. Christmas dinner the next day would be turkey, roast potatoes, sprouts, cranberry sauce and a good claret. My daughter and her husband, who live in Okehampton, are traditionalists. Chris and I tend to be salad and a slice of quiche people, but that's the way it goes these days. You go forward into a quicker, lighter future and the children hop off backwards into the past, staring at you and muttering 'Weird.' But we love to see our daughter, and we have a new grandchild, and our son and his new fiancée would be joining us.

We'd finished work in Amsterdam and had a host of presents already wrapped, which we'd packed into the suitcase, so we could just trolley them out at the Bristol end and then head straight down the M5. Yes, very clever. Well organized. My husband does all that. It's his thing, dates and timetables and being at the right place at the right time, and I trot along behind. He does consultancy work for a Dutch property company. I'm a writer; I fit in.

Too clever by half, of course. We'd reckoned without Christmas, or at any rate Yuletide. We'd reckoned without the waywardness of humanity. We'd not taken into account the seasonal urgency which sometimes catches us up like a tide, so we move as others do, in a group, and do what we must, not what reason says. Princess Diana's funeral, trolley rage at the supermarket just before the bank holiday . . . It was just the same when Thor cracked his thunder over northern skies and everyone jumped the same way at his command. Rituals must be observed. They have their own imperative.

Amsterdam is far enough north to still be partly the land of the Nordic gods, and Christmas is still Yuletide, their midwinter festival. I have always suspected Schiphol Airport to be Thor's own place, all that cracking of the skies, the low thunder of aircraft breaking through the clouds, the tremble of the ground as the big jets land. Thor likes it; he hangs around. This year Christmas Day falls on a Thursday (*donderag* in Dutch), his day—all the more likely for him to put in an appearance. When the god roars out over the flat damp land, saying that it's time to shut the doors and bring out the drink, people do as he says, and who cares what the timetables say?

We got early to the airport and checked in the luggage. We'd allowed ourselves twenty minutes to look round the Rijksmuseum annexe before going to the gate. We like to do that. There is something refreshing, like cool clear water on a hot day, about looking at paintings in an airport. It restores you to sanity. There's currently an exhibition of Rembrandt prints which Chris particularly wanted to catch. But my attention was caught by a farmyard painting by Melchior d'Hondecoeter, 1636–1695. Two vain and disdainful peacocks look down their nose at a little, pretty, silly hen with four fluffy chicks, while a great gobbling turkey, stupid and amazed, looks on. I wondered which of them was most like me. I asked Chris, hoping, I suppose, for some kind of compliment or reassurance, but instead of answering he said, 'We can't be too long here. We don't want to miss our flight. Shall we go?'

Now I can't bear to be hurried. Chris can't bear to be late. And I was feeling tetchy— Christmas brings out the worst in me, not the best. I was tired. The trouble with family is you have to work so very hard at not saying the wrong thing. 'Don't panic,' I said, meanly. 'You are so neurotic about time. They have our luggage, they can't go without us.' And for once I didn't relieve him of his anxiety by consenting to leave at once, but lingered and let him fret. It is the kind of cruelty that even the fondest couples sometimes practise— putting the other person in the wrong, pressing their buttons. It may fall short of an outright row, but it verges on one.

The elegant girl from the Rijksmuseum shop, the only member of staff left on the premises, was beginning to hover and look at her watch. That irritated me too. I am a customer; I have my rights. It was only ten past three; there were five full minutes before the place was due to close for the six days of the Christmas holiday. I was looking at Art. I shouldn't be hurried.

It was almost twenty past three by the time we left and the poor thing could hiss the doors shut behind us. She stalked past us as we left, long legged. She carried crimson and gold parcels, prettily tied with Rijksmuseum ribbon. She was one of the peacocks, disdainful.

In the space of fifteen minutes Schiphol had stopped being a busy, noisy, excited place and become a lonely expanse of empty walkways. Shops had closed, passengers gone their ways. Lights were muted. Even the all-pervasive smell of coffee was fading. 'Yuletide!' said the notices, 'Happy Christmas! Bon Noël!' But here and there 'New Year Sale' signs had gone up.

The passport booth was closed and empty. Barriers were up. We had to find another one, and the Information desk was closed. The moving walkway slowed and stopped while we were on it. The languid warning voice dropped a tone and droned and was silent. We ran. Even I ran. We ran down a flight of steps—the escalator had stopped—to gate C4, where our flight was closing. Even as we ran we heard a gate change. Now it was gate C6. We ran some more.

And then we sat, because when we got there, there was no urgency, the flight was delayed. One minute we were racing, the next we were staring into space. Airports are like that. And we sat, and sat and sat.

'We could have taken our time,' said Chris. He is very good. He could have said earlier, as we ran, 'Told you so.' But he didn't.

There were six of us: one little old lady who had been drinking, one shabby businessman who looked as if he had been up all night and a young engaged couple. She was plump and blonde and fidgety and reminded me of the busy little hen in the painting. He was the turkey, cross and awkward, with a nose too big and a chin too small. But he loved her. He kept trying to hold her hand, but she pushed him away. She was upset. There were tears in her eyes. I don't know what they had quarrelled about but it seemed quite bad. Two hours passed.

Pretty soon I had tears in my eyes too. The flight had been cancelled. There had been a technical fault. Thor was punishing me. I had been mean to Chris; I had been mean to the girl in the shop. I had not heeded the clarion call to the midwinter ritual. The last flights to Heathrow had gone. There was no way we could leave Schiphol that night. It was Christmas Eve. They were running a skeleton service. They would put us up in the airport hotel. They apologized for the inconvenience caused. We would be compensated. No, luggage could not be returned. It was already on the aircraft. There had been an industrial dispute and the baggage handlers had gone home.

There was a strange underwater feeling to everything. I could hear Schiphol breathing—or was it the air conditioning in the great echoey empty halls? In and out, very slowly. Thor's breath. The airline staff were very polite, very thoughtful, but they too were looking at their watches. Everyone wanted to be off. It was Christmas.

We were all silent. 'A Fokker F150,' said the businessman, looking out of the window as our plane taxied away, cute and antsy. As if the make made a difference. There was a crack of thunder from outside and lightning—only two seconds between the two—but no rain. 'Two propellers,' he observed. I think he was stunned. So was I. 'Nice little aircraft. Cityhopper. Doesn't usually go wrong.' But it was no use to us.

The blonde girl, whose name was Penny, threw her engagement ring across the floor. It skittered and bounced. The boy, whose name was Darrell, set his jaw and didn't go after it.

'That's it,' said Penny. 'That's it.'

'Yes, it is,' said Darrell. 'Goodbye you and goodbye Christmas.'

It seemed a great pity to me, the way the whole world had to suffer from the weight of my sin. The ring glittered under a plastic chair. I thought it was a diamond. The old lady said it was all right by her, she didn't like Christmas anyway. I longed to be at home in bed.

They bussed us to the airport hotel. The rain broke as we stood outside waiting for it to arrive. We were soaked. Thor was letting me know who ran things round here. I had no face cream; Chris had no sleeping pills. The young couple still weren't talking. I was distressed for them. It seemed such a waste of life. I was sure neither of them would find anyone better. I told Chris so. He said it was projection; personally, he was distressed for *us*.

The hotel was crowded. Industrial dispute, fog and storm had wreaked havoc with flights. They gave us tickets so we could be called in order to the reception desk. Someone from the airline came over and said they would try to get us out first thing the next morning. Christmas Day. She was the other peacock, the disdainful type.

'Now I must be off,' she said. 'In Holland we take Christmas Eve seriously. It is our most important festival.'

We made phone calls. We said, 'Don't expect us tonight, we've been delayed, we'll be in touch when we know more.' We were past caring about having no night things. There were plates of free food in the bar, but I wasn't hungry. Chris gnawed on a chicken leg. Our numbers came up. There was one room left, a double. They gave it to Chris and me. Everyone else would have to sleep in armchairs and on sofas in the lobby. I said to Chris, 'Please can we give the room to them,' meaning the young couple, and he looked at them and looked at me and said, 'Okay.' He is not a man of many words. We slept and partly slept, and outside the storm died down.

In the morning everyone said 'Happy Christmas' to each other, and there was big notice up with an arrow saying 'Yuletide breakfast this way', and there was, too, fresh bread and good coffee and fine eggs. The young couple came down from the bedroom. They had made it up. They smiled soppily at everyone. Chris looked in his pocket and handed them the ring. He had actually stopped to pick it up.

The young couple leant into each other in the Cityhopper, the Fokker F150, all the way home. An oil seal had been mended. We had missed Christmas Eve goose and our hire car, but my son-in-law would pick us up and we'd be in time for Christmas lunch. We even had the presents with us.

'Look at you!' said Chris, as we disembarked into brilliant morning sun, 'you're smarter than a peacock, nicer than a mother hen, and not one bit like the turkey,' and I glowed, and marvelled at the rich splendour of the world.

Moral

Nothing is as good as you hope or
as bad as you fear.

Food

The Fleeting Happiness Food Brings

Next to sex, food, being such a basic source of the most wonderful pleasure, is also the most basic source of exquisite anxiety and all-pervasive guilt.

Wanting to eat is instinctive. It's like sex—you find yourself wanting to do it. If you didn't want to, you wouldn't do it, and you'd starve to death, as anorexics do.

Anorexics lack the urge to eat and eat some more, before the winter comes and there's only the fat you stored in the summer to get you through the hungry days. Anorexics are out of touch with their species selves. They are all mind and soul, spiritual, brides of Christ, rejecting the flesh.

Bulimics are all instinct: eat and eat and eat, and only when the craving's stopped do mind and soul cut in, and by vomiting demonstrate repentance.

The person with the food disorder cannot get the balance right. Bulimic and anorexic swap and interchange. Nature says, *'Eat.'* Nurture says, *'Don't. Thin is best.'*

Eat for ten minutes and then feel the anxiety begin. *'How many calories was that?'* Now the guilt. *'Was I mad? Did I just eat strawberry jam?'*

Bananas

I looked in the fruit bowl just now and found a bunch of bananas, rapidly going brown from lack of anyone's interest. (I try to eat one a day, to keep my potassium levels up, but keep forgetting.) It seemed a pity to waste them. So I took the over-ripe bananas, peeled them, sliced them in two down the middle, criss-crossed the halves in an oven dish, added butter and sugar, and slid them into a very hot oven. Thirty minutes later I removed the dish and squeezed lemon juice over the now caramelized, buttery, amazingly interesting bananas.

I put them to one side. The struggle with the self began. *'Should I eat them? Shouldn't I eat them?'* Food makes you fat. It also keeps you alive.

I thought about adding ice-cream: cold and hot together add to the taste buds' delight. But I had run out. The double cream in the fridge was well beyond its sell-by date and smelled bitter.

There is no diet in the world which will allow you to eat banana, sugar, butter and lemon juice, forget cream, at the same time, and at will. And in quantity, because one spoonful of the disallowed will always lead to another.

Three Types

We fall broadly into three different physical types:

Endomorphs: rounded and happy

Ectomorphs: skinny and anxious

Mesomorphs: athletic, muscly and busy

No one's going to be wholly one thing or another, but the predominant traits are going to be visible to everyone. You can have the sharp elbows of the ectomorph, the muscular calves of the mesomorph and the double chin of the endomorph all on one body—and God help you. But one type will be favoured.

You will mostly find endomorphs (I'm one) on the Atkins diet, on which you're allowed to drink alcohol and eat everything that in your previous dietary life has been forbidden. It is also probably going to ruin your health and make you ill (what do you care) and you will put it all back on (fine) and more (not so fine). Atkins dieters are self-indulgent and always hopeful. Their self-discipline is not good. They run to fat around the middle. They should certainly not be eating caramelized bananas cooked to stop good fruit going to waste.

Mesomorphs, in my experience, go on GI diets. They're the healthy-looking, broad-shouldered, narrow-waisted energetic girls you see in the gym, especially on the weights. Everything they eat will be healthy, reasonable and balanced. They would look first at the caramelized bananas and then at you as if you were insane. They're the ones who lose weight successfully. They're the broad-shouldered healthy-looking celebrities, the film stars who have their babies and six weeks later you'd never have known it.

Ectomorphs would smell the aroma of the caramelized bananas, run it to its source and simply reach out and eat every scrap, having restocked on ice-cream and charmed a (male) neighbour into lending them some cream first. They're skinny and they have long legs and they eat everything and never get fat. See them putting aside their hamburgers before shimmying down the catwalk. See them sitting in reception while the mesomorphs haul the post and the endomorphs hide behind the filing cabinets. (Mind you, it can be quite exciting back there—think President Clinton and Monica Lewinsky, an endomorph if ever there was one.)

Now that a girl can have a boob job to order and small breasts need no longer bother her, contentment should be complete.

But it isn't. Species inheritance affects all physical types. Anxiety and guilt strike all of us, though ectomorphs least of all when it comes to food.

Personally, I capitulate to the bananas. Of course I do. I eat. I leave a bit on the plate and then think, *'What the hell,'* and go on and finish the lot. I am an endomorph. I prefer present pleasure to future benefit. (I may also be a bit more inclined to depression than my mesomorph and ectomorph sisters, so have less sense of future than they do. Sure, if I don't eat this I will be thinner *then*, but this is *now, now, now.)*

Nothing, I know from experience, is more delicious than caramelized bananas eaten in the privacy of one's own home. It's like forbidden sex—all the more delicious for the prohibition.

I eat. I am happy for three minutes. Yummy!

Then, oh, guilt and anxiety dawning! I have enjoyed myself. I don't deserve to be happy. I will be punished. I shouldn't have bought the bananas in the first place if I didn't mean to eat them properly.

And what was that I heard myself saying? *Yummy?* Revolting. I remember the girl who used to come in to help with my children, years back, and how she'd rub my three-year-old's tummy after he'd eaten and say, *'Yummy.'* I never liked it. There was something somehow wrong with it. She might give him a weight problem for life—too much emphasis on the *'Yummy'* content of food and not enough on the *'Swallow it down and get on with it.'*

I was right. It transpired that she was having an affair with my then husband.

And now I feel sick, and serve me right.

Eat, Eat

It is no use beating yourself up, reproaching yourself about being greedy. That is what you are. That is what you are born to be. *'Eat!'* says nature. *'Eat!'* You do.

The eye sees the food!

The hand takes the food!

The mouth eats the food!

The teeth chew it!

That's what they have all evolved to do!

At the same time it is not good to be fat. Bad news in the mating game—nurture in the form of our socialization has seen to that. Slim wins the alpha male, fat gets the leftovers. But you have to eat to be fit enough to bear a baby, even though you want to be thin to get the best mate. Two instincts clash. You suffer.

There's no fairness here, either. Some women can be as greedy as they like and stay thin:

Ectomorphs, who are lucky. Born thin and nervy, they stay thin and nervy. They can live off fish and chips and Mars bars if they want.

Mesomorphs, the born exercisers. They put on weight and take it off again, down the gym. It works for them.

Endomorphs are unlucky all round. Born plump and placid and prone to depression, they are also the least likely to diet successfully.

But they're the ones people like to have around. When nature and nurture clash in them, nature plainly wins. And those in whom instinct triumphs tend to be nicer people than those in whom it is subdued. They're spontaneous and loveable.

But I would say that, wouldn't I? I'm an endomorph.

Still, fat people are the nicest people, and increasingly in the West the *most* people. Perhaps, just as Mother Nature puts berries on the yew trees to warn of a cold winter ahead, she makes us fat to warn us of hard times to come?

That's the kind of myth the tribe likes. It doesn't really bear investigation. It's what is called the pathetic fallacy, attributing emotions, intent and the power of prophecy to a force incapable of it, namely 'nature'. But it's nice to speculate.

It's also nice to be nice. And to be thin. The tribe unites in making fat people unwelcome, uncomfortable. So nice people are not necessarily the happiest people.

Moral

Be good about the diet and you'll
be happy to be thin.

At the Mercy of our Greed

The eating of food being such a pleasure, so hardwired and yet so in conflict with society's current loathing of fat, it is not surprising the conflict tears us to pieces. Body mass index not within normal limits? *'Hang your head in shame, you fat person.'* Guilt and anxiety race in almost after the first mouthful of delight. As if life wasn't hard enough without this.

Did evolution stop just before the first good harvest? Is that it? Before the age of plenty? To all intents and purposes, yes. Evolution bred greed into us—*'Take while you can, as much as you can, who knows when it will come again?'*—and the pleasure of satisfying appetite—*'Oh yummy, yummy'*—and the yawning repletion of appetite satisfied—*'My, that was good!'* It has not yet had time to evolve us into persons fit for the age of McDonald's. That may take another millennium or two, left to nature, but no doubt the genetic scientists will get there first and turn us into a race of skinnies who can eat what they like and still stay acceptable in polite society. (When no doubt the plankton will dry up, there'll be a universal food shortage, women will long for curves and the scientists will have to return us to what we once were.)

As it is, lumbered with *now*, as we are, nature says, *'Forage, cook, feed the man who keeps the children fed. Keep strong, keep fat.'* Nurture says, *'Push away the plate half-eaten. You keep the children fed yourself, you don't need him. Keep thin, welcome hunger—the skinnier you are, the more you'll get paid at the office.'*

(*Fact:* Obesity lowers perceived status. The higher your status, the longer you live and the healthier you are. A vicious circle. Being fat is associated with poverty, depression, ignorance and being on benefit. Being slim is associated with the Duchess of Windsor: *'You can't be too rich or too thin.'* The phrase has stuck, 70 years or so after it was uttered by the runaway would-be queen Wallis Simpson, because everyone believes it to be true—other than the families of anorexics, who are in great distress.)

Nurture and nature, which should in a perfect world go hand in hand, when it comes to food simply do not. It's not surprising that the country is in the grip of one big eating problem. The more we feel distaste for being fat, the more cookery books we read. The more we long to be thin, the more obese we get, as we try to comfort ourselves, deny cause and effect.

Fashion also dictates that thin is best. Being slim is associated with wealth, choice and purchasing power. Designers challenge us, *'Fit into our clothes. Don't expect us to make clothes to fit you.'*

Way Out

If you feel guilty and anxious about eating, stop eating. Who are you trying to destroy there? Yourself?

Easily said—and people say it—but the trouble is that food breeds anxiety, and anxiety requires food to quell it. It is a vicious circle. But people do break it.

Remember what research tells us: that skinny women earn more than fat women, marry richer husbands, have more lovers, go to smarter restaurants and die with more jewellery. They wear more designer clothes than fat women and look far, far better in them.

(Tallness is to men as skinniness is to women. Tall men earn more, live longer, marry prettier and nicer wives, have more lovers and go to smarter restaurants than short men. They tend not to accumulate so much jewellery, though.)

So be thin.

Convince yourself it's winter and there's simply no food to be had. That it's an eternal winter. That you can take it.

Remember, oh unfortunate endomorphs, with your legs shorter than your torsos and your tendency to run to fat around the middle, how great is your achievement if you manage to get thin and stay thin. Mesomorphs, luckier in that they can exercise and lose weight with comparative ease (though their ribcages will stay wide), deserve some credit. Ectomorphs, you fragile, lightly muscled things, elegantly and effortlessly slim, realize that though for you summer is always here, the rest of us can't afford to think like that. You see us as greedy, without self-control. You don't *understand.*

The way through again, if I could venture so outrageous an idea, lies not in this diet or that, but in seeking virtue. Not, *'Oh, I've eaten no carbohydrates today, aren't I good?'* or *'Oh, I've eaten lots of carbohydrates today, aren't I good?'*, but to go back to the old idea of our great-grandparents, that the body is the temple of the soul, and the preoccupation should be looking after the soul rather than the body. Not *'What will this food do to me?'* but *'How will this food benefit the temple?'*

It is your duty to look after the temple. Keep it not too fat, not too thin, not inviting ill-health, well exercised, allowed its proper pleasures, indulged a little but not too much—in as perfect and cheerful a state as age will permit it to be. Pursue a fit shelter for the soul and the body will look after itself.

Friends

It's natural to have friends. You feel unhappy and lonely if you don't. The tribe troops together to keep danger at bay. It exchanges information, ideas, experience. That way survival lies.

In particular women need other women. If only to act as midwives.

We may live in cities, but we are still people of the tribe. We tend to cluster in our own age group:

Little girls congregate to discuss their frilly socks.

Teenagers get together to work out their seduction techniques.

Singletons go to the cinema in giggling groups.

Young mothers meet up in the park.

Older women meet for lunch.

Yet older women talk on the landline.

And the fun to be had is immeasurable, and

the level of anxiety and guilt low.

Of course little girls squabble and brood, teenagers plot, singletons get competitive, younger mothers can be bitchy. Older women can decide never to speak to you again for reasons only known to them. Yet older women can forget all about you, through no fault of their own. But by and large having friends seems to be an activity encouraged and unconflicted by instinct. Nature encourages it as part of the cohesion of the tribe.

When a man turns up, as everyone knows, everything changes. Women complain the spark goes out of the party. It's not the spark, it's that something judgemental enters in— nature reminding us of our destiny, our obligation to the future. It isn't worse. It's just different.

Sure, the mating game takes precedence. Any sensible girl stands up her friends when a hot date comes galloping over the hill.

I know it is irritating to speak as if women were people who had babies, and that was their only definition, but Mother Nature is hopelessly old-fashioned. That's how she sees them, doling out the oestrogen like nobody's business. She does it in dollops. If she makes a mistake, and it's not rare, she'll dollop out testosterone to a girl in the womb, and she'll grow up to be an astronaut or an engineer. Good for her. She won't be unhappy. She'll just earn more.

The girl who at 13 is a clumsy stolid loaf of lard can turn suddenly into a bright-eyed, attractive, shapely lass. That's oestrogen. Now she's ready for the mating game. Nature says now, and makes her silly, vulnerable and sexy.

Our genes dictate when enough is enough and we're to stop producing oestrogen. Our skin dries out, our waists thicken, we are post-menopausal. We get depressed, overlooked and disregarded by the still fertile. We are fit for nature's scrap heap.

Fortunately, not for society's.

Nature also gave us brains surplus to our survival requirements and the ability to get round her strictures. We add the stuff artificially. We're back in business.

Nature doesn't care. Nature doesn't know. Nature is blind, deaf and dumb. Following her strictures in the modern world is pretty pointless. All she knows about is Darwinian evolution. She knows nothing about the soul.

The Pleasure of Friends

You can do without partners, husbands, lovers, children, jobs and money, so long as you have good friends. It is advisable to try to accumulate the others as you go through life, because then happiness is maximized, but you can do without if you have to.

In the good times friends are fun. They're to laugh with, drink with, eat with and refine ideas with. They're the mini-tribe you set up around you.

In the bad times friends are essential. They take you to hospital, give you a bed for the night, take in your children and lend you money. They listen to you for hours on the phone when you're in distress.

You do the same for them, or should. Be good to your friends and they'll be good to you.

No one's life is so in control that they know what's going to happen next. Aircraft fall out of the sky, tsunamis hit, husbands have heart attacks, children get meningitis. Friends turn up trumps.

For the most part friends make you happy. They can also betray you, give you bad advice, lie to you and tell tales about you out of school. They can spread malice and dissent.

They can turn out to be still 13 at heart and decide to persecute you.

I had one good friend who I think somehow got me mixed up with her string of husbands. Left without one temporarily, she decided to divorce me. Losing friends is very painful.

Friends are powerful people. They can influence you too much, especially if you're at the courting stage in life. The gaggle of teenage girls, noisy and defiant, crude and lewd, is nothing alarming, not the end of civilization as we know it, it's just more tribal behaviour, only nowadays with the help of sex, drink and drugs. The process was the same in Victorian days. Young girls gather together in groups, working out their relationships with each other, trying out their own gender for size, as it were, before starting on men. One by one they peel away to create families of their own. Or should. The group can get over-possessive and destructive.

Intent is all. Motive matters.

Tell your best friend her new boyfriend is crap, she can do better than that, and next time he calls she'll put down the phone. Or might, at least. So only say it if it's true, not because she's the one who helps fill your own lonely evenings, because you shop together, go clubbing together, because her mother gives you tea and sympathy and you don't want to lose her.

It's not what you say, but the reason you say it that counts. And people sense it, and like you or leave you accordingly.

I have a rich and fashionable acquaintance who sees friends as social accessories. Once a year she gives herself a birthday party. She flies the 'friends' in from all over the world. It costs her a bomb. This is the only time she ever sees them. She makes an emotional speech after dinner and talks about how many friends she has and how they have supported her and how important they are in her life. Everyone feels warm and friendly. Then they all go away and she is left with the cook, the butler and the personal trainer, who are her real friends, but do not, of course, get asked to dinner.

Well, why not? If this is how she wants to spend her money, good for her. 'Friends' are whatever you define them as. I tend to define mine as the people who wander into the house and collapse exhausted and distraught at the kitchen table, but each to their own.

I read in the paper that anyone who has six friends can call themselves 'happy'. I can do that easily, if I include the guy who sells the

Big Issue outside the supermarket. We always smile and say good day. And e-mail makes good colleagues of us all.

But already I'm worrying. Why haven't I heard from Wendy? Have I said something to upset her? And I should have called Stacey for the latest on her heart procedure, but it went out of my head. Anxious, guilty? But usually with friendships these are quickly allayed:

> If the anxiety is of the free-floating variety and can be applied to this circumstance or that, breathe deeply and dismiss it. *'No, you have not upset Wendy. Stacey doesn't expect a phone call.'*

> If the Wendy guilt is reasonable—you told her to stop moaning, it was getting on your nerves—*call and apologize.* Don't text—in these circumstances it's an evasion.

> If the Stacey guilt is well founded, *call her and find out what's happening.* The longer you leave it, the worse it will get.

Let me tell you a parable about a girl who knew she was better than others, knew she was right, and made sure others knew it too. She kept to the rules and made sure everyone else did too, and it did her no good.

It's another Christmas story because it's at Christmas, or whatever mid-winter festival we keep, that we tend to meet ourselves as we really are.

Sometimes I Feel Like Crying

I like Christmas Eve. The office closes at midday. I reckon to get all my Christmas shopping done in the few hours available before the big stores shut. That's usually around 4.00 or 4.30. Colleagues marvel at my efficiency, but I explain it's just a question of being organized.

'It's not that I'm so great,' I say, 'it's just that you lot are so inefficient: you worry and fret and get neurotic. All you have to do is forward plan, know exactly what you mean to buy and go to any big department store of which you have previously obtained a floor map. By leaving it to the last moment too, you can save money. By 24 December the stores are setting up for the post-Christmas sales, a lot of stuff is already marked as reduced and sales staff are too exhausted by the seasonal long hours to keep up any argument that everything is meant to be full price until Boxing Day. "Marked down is marked down," say I, and they capitulate.'

It's not that I'm mean, you understand. I just

don't like spending money unnecessarily. I see so much of it. I work for a large insurance company, monitoring claims. This year I was promoted to head of department. I take the responsibility seriously. People waste so much money just because they can't be bothered to read the small print. It appals me. I'm sorry for them sometimes, but what can I do? So an owl flies in an open window and leaves a nasty trail across the wedding feast, including the cake, and you put in a claim. 'But bird damage is specifically excluded in your agreement,' I say. 'You get nothing.'

There it is, bold as brass, in the small print. Well, 'bold' might not be quite the word—I reckon the font's about eight—but there it is all the same.

'But I've spent £900 a year for the last 15 years on insurance and never claimed a thing,' comes the response. 'Now my daughter's wedding is ruined. Is this all you can do for me?'

And all I can say is 'Sorry, you should have read the agreement before you signed it.' I think before my promotion I might have stretched a point—we do have some discretion—but not now. I see my duty as being to my employers.

Mind you, the toy department can be a bit tricky by Christmas Eve. Things do sell out, and one may have to revise one's list pretty quickly, but there's always the educational toys to fall back upon. If staff act reluctant and say, 'But it's so late, Parcel Collection in the basement must just about be closing,' I remind them of their Christmas ads and put it to them that they don't want to be in contravention of the Trades Descriptions Act. The whole store is advertised as open, not just bits of it. They soon enough find a messenger to take whatever it is first to gift-wrapping then down to the basement to await collection.

A ceiling of £10 a present and ten presents to buy and that's exactly £100 for Christmas, plus train fares home to my parents for the family get-together. Not bad. I book the train well in advance to make sure I get a good reduction. If there's any nonsense I demand that they call head office and get the management to read them the small print on discounted fares. It's best to book such tickets in person, in the rush hour. A long queue behind you, pressing for attention, usually brings results.

Anyway, at 4.26, gift-shopping complete and only £89 spent, it was time to turn my attention to me. I went on up to the Bargain

Bin on the third floor—that's Fashion—to look for a glitzy top to wear with my jeans for the New Year's party. I have just about a perfect figure—34, 26, 34—which I've dieted and exercised and liposuctioned to achieve, so most things look okay on me, they don't have to be expensive.

I found a piece of really agreeable glitter, low cut to make the most of the 34. It was reduced from £90 to £8—not bad at all. I do rather rely on the New Year's party to find my escort for the year. Around September I tend to get fed up with them and say goodbye, then I give myself three months solo in which to firm up my friendships. That done, my bed begins to feel a little empty and by Christmas I'm quite looking forward to filling it with someone new. I'm only 28, too young to settle down.

As it happens, last year's escort actually dumped me before I could dump him, and that's made me nervous. His name was Corin.

'I don't know what's the matter with you, Jacqui,' he said as he walked out. 'Every day you seem to get meaner and tougher. Perhaps it's your job.'

I am not tough, I am not mean, I am just

practical and hate waste. If anything, I'm too soft. I even trained as a nurse. My heart bled for humanity—so much so I had to give up because of the stress. Now at least suffering humanity only comes to me through the post, or at the end of a phone if reception slips up and lets the calls through.

I should be feeling happy and relaxed, here in the bosom of my loving family, at the time of year I most love, in that blissful torpor that descends on the land between Christmas and the New Year, when the office is closed and the streets are empty and you have time to have baths and read books and think about yourself. I don't often do that. There isn't time, is there? I often work a twelve-hour day.

Yet for some reason I feel like crying. I've turned soft and gentle. See what just five days away from the office can do for a girl? I sit in my childhood bedroom looking out over the bare garden and think of Corin. I miss him.

I can hear my mother pottering about in the living room below, doing her annual lament at the too-early falling of the Christmas tree needles, and my father tangling with the streamers as ever, and my twin nieces and one nephew arguing over their toys.

103

I don't know how my sister Effie had the courage to have children; I don't know how any woman has. You have no control whatsoever over what comes out, and no insurance. If ever I have children I'll have them by cloning, thank you very much. Fortunately Effie's kids seem just about okay and I love them and they love me.

But anyway, my gold top. I had quite a tussle with this particular sales girl. She had greasy blonde hair with black roots. She said the top had got into the Bargain Bin by mistake and was a designer piece and the asking price was £900 and I had to pay the shelf price. That was absurd. Black-roots was temporary Christmas staff; they can be greater sticklers than the regular girls. I noticed her hand was trembling. I knew then I would win.

I demanded to see the manager, and when Black-roots claimed she'd already have gone home, inasmuch as the store was now closed, I said oh no the store wasn't, not while my stuff was down in the basement waiting for me to turn up. First I made her call down to Parcel Collection to confirm that they understood this. Then I made her come with me to the managerial level on the sixth floor and we banged on doors until we found some woman still packing up, who, after I had explained the situation in detail, said, 'Oh give it to her for £8, for God's sake just give it to her,' and we went downstairs. When I said I wanted the top gift-wrapped Black-roots began to cry and I relented and said, 'Okay, just shove it in any old bag,' and she did. I do have a kind heart. I even said, 'I do hope you get to the hairdresser before tomorrow, so you can get your roots done.'

It was 5.10 by the time the janitor had unlocked Parcel Collection—can you imagine, they'd just shut up shop and gone home, their business unfinished? I would never have done a thing like that. As a result I actually missed my train and had to get the next one, and you can imagine what happened next. The conductor said my ticket wasn't valid on the train, I argued that it was the crowds on the platform as result of a couple of their cancelled trains that had held me up, so it was the railway company's fault, not mine. I got my way, but only after a short unscheduled stop while the transport police were called, and somehow I didn't feel the normal stab of triumph. In fact I felt rather depressed. Why is everything always so uphill?

If I go on getting value for money like this, I will have the deposit of a house saved within a year. But who will there be to help me with the mortgage? No lovers in sight and friends pretty thin on the ground. My bright idea for giving up smoking was never to buy cigarettes but always to ask others for them and let social embarrassment stand between me and the wasteful, unhealthy habit. But I think my s.e. threshold is rather high. It must be. I smoked just as many cigarettes and ended up with fewer friends.

Downstairs someone opens a window.

'Now all the robots are broken,' one of the twins is saying, 'we've only got what Auntie Bug Meanie gave us.' Me, Auntie Bug Meanie?

'Hush. She'll hear,' says my sister. 'We don't want to upset her.'

'Why not?' asks the niece, in the manner of small children.

'She's upset enough as it is,' says my sister, and I suppose that's true. Since Corin walked out I've been unhappy. I haven't seen why other people should be having a good time when I'm not.

My father says I've grown obsessive about money, but he's a fine one to talk. He's a gambler, he spends money obsessively, the way I save it. And they even make him pay an entrance fee to get into their bloody casino. I'd never stand for that. He's too soft.

I begin to cry. Time stretches forward and back in an odd way. Forward to the New Year's Eve party where I just might meet Mr Right, with the aid of a gold top which I should have paid £900 for and paid £8. Back to Christmas Eve when I bought it, and that poor girl with the black roots crying. I hope she got to the hairdresser. Bet she didn't. And then Christmas Day, and my mother opening her diary and my father his wallet—you can get both in leather goods—and my sister her gardening gloves and my brother in law his secateurs—both from gardening, the next section along—and the children their educational gifts, just down the escalator, and all their faces as they opened them, and how the adults seemed both polite and somehow concerned, and the children just plain unbelieving.

It's true that once I was famous for the originality and extravagance of my presents and would never, never have had a store gift-wrap anything. It would be all wicked paper wrap and coloured string and tags and bows and glitter and so forth, done by me. And I wondered what was happening to me.

I call Corin on his mobile. I know the number

by heart, though it's been six months since we split.

'I think you're right,' I said. 'I blame my job. If they pay you to be mean and tough, that's what you become. If you get paid for reading the small print, you get into the habit.'

There was silence at the other end of the phone. Then Corin said, 'You could try blaming yourself.'

So I put the phone down. He was a pompous prat. I'd quite got over him. But I thought I might call by the store and leave a box of chocolates for Black-roots. She might even become my friend. I might even, who knows, chuck in my job and go back to nursing. Try living by the small print and everyone hates you. I give up.

Moral

If you let life and times work upon you, if you can listen to what is being said to you, and reform—and indeed repent—you will have your reward.

I can tell you that Black-roots, whose real name was Rachel, did indeed become Jacqui's friend. They went out for a coffee and Rachel told

Jacqui that to have black roots was purposeful, trendy and a gesture of defiance to her employers. 'They don't like it,' she said, 'but no way can they fire you.'

Jacqui had her own hair done the same. It was easy. You get your hair bleached all over and then just wait for nature to run its course. By the time the roots were an inch deep Corin was back, and liked Jacqui's new style. He could see that she was loosening up.

Jacqui is not the warmest of people, though she shows promise. She felt remorse and acted upon it. All the same she needs her soul strengthening to make her truly likeable. There are exercises which can be done. Treat the soul, like the brain, in the same way as you would a muscle. To make it stronger, use it.

Rachel could join Jacqui in a quest for culture, and general elevation of the spirit. The more you perceive the difference between the mundane and the divine, the more responsive you become to the latter.

Exercises to Strengthen the Soul

Seek exposure to the arts, since they are God given.

(The Darwinians deny it, I have to admit. No God, they claim. No intelligent design, no supreme Maker, not even one who set the clock of the universe ticking. Music and dance are survival friendly, that's all. Art is sympathetic magic, cave painting just part of the religious ritual of fools. Literature likewise—random variations on the holy books of the primitives. These claims may be true, but other things are true as well.)

Exposure to the arts refines the spirit. Exposure to what is best in the arts increases our resistance to the shoddy, the brash, the ugly. If you listen to music long enough and hard enough, you can just about hear the music of the spheres. If you look at enough paintings, you will automatically choose the least offensive sofa in the shop.

All those parents trailing their unwilling children around art galleries do them a great service. Those who see only what is ugly—concrete and graffiti—grow up to be ugly of spirit and negligible of soul.

Certain shopping malls clear their centres of hoods by playing Bach over the sound system: vampires scatter when presented with a cross. Think about it.

Exercise 1: Go to a Concert

Jacqui and Rachel need to go to a concert. They've mostly only ever heard muzak, or sound delivered directly into their brains via iPod, which drives out any possibility of reflection. Like a hot, hot wind the iPod dries out and shrivels the tender green shoot of a growing soul. Silence now makes them nervous.

A Beethoven string quartet at the Wigmore Hall would be a good shock introduction, but perhaps too much of one. Jacqui and Rachel could only marvel at how it was that so many delicate and refined-looking people—women with long earrings, men with ridiculous large glasses—could sit for so long, listening to the screeching of strings? Tell them that the audience strains to hear the music of paradise and all they'll say is 'weird'.

A night out at the Proms would be less rarefied, and perhaps more advisable; the 169 golden angels on the Albert Memorial could waft them through the great doors of the hall, and the rolls of drums and the suggestion of a tune, though only now and then, might pacify them enough to make them stay. And perhaps if they listened hard enough they might just hear the music of the spheres and exult. It is not beyond the bounds of possibility. Exultation is to the soul as Baby Bio is to the Busy Lizzie.

Failing that, let them go to any concert—rock, pop or hip hop. At least live music disturbs the air and is a real and not a virtual thing, and sharing tunes with the like-minded can do your soul no actual harm. Jacqui needs to feel herself at one with others, not just a reader of the small print but part of a whole which might start in Hyde Park but stretches and stretches to include Great Britain, the world, the universe and all creation. Awe is what the soul feeds upon.

Exercise 2: Go to a Gallery

Jacqui and Rachel can cross London and go to the National Gallery. Their eyes will no doubt glaze over at first. They will want to go to the café and to the shop, but won't find much they want to take home, let alone wear. It's all so middle-aged and middle class.

But a poster of a Van Gogh chair quite takes their eye. It is the one used to advertise the gallery. It is the same chair which hangs in one of the galleries upstairs, essence of chair—woven rush seat, yellow painted wood, tiled floor, blue curtain—but put through a clever technological process for the benefit of the gallery promotion, distorted until it seems to be somehow liquidizing. Demons might laugh with joy to see it.

Jacqui and Rachel stare at the poster a little bit. 'That's wicked,' says Rachel, accurately enough. But Jacqui has a vague memory from school that it's not really like that and they trip all the way up the stairs and through the tourist throng to see the original. Jacqui's right. The chair is not liquidizing. It's still there, as ever, solid, imposing its vision on posterity. 'I prefer this one,' Jacqui says, and angels dance, and pin a gold star on her soul, or whatever they do, just to encourage it.

On the way down the steps Jacqui has a strange pain in her heart and tears come into her eyes and she can't think why. It's the sudden sharpness of the pin, no doubt.

Exercise 3: Go to Church

Not some dreary place of worship, the pews gone and chairs put in their place, fixed together for easy handling so they creak when you move, with bongo drums, jingle music, social worker vicar and counselling after the service, but a proper old-fashioned church. They could try Westminster Abbey.

They might be impressed by its ancient magnificence, the idea that their forebears felt at home in such places, went to extraordinary efforts to afford and build them, to the greater glory of God. They might be moved by sheer marvel to take their iPods out. They might even stay to a service, with any luck in the old-fashioned language, which you can only half-understand, but in the half-understanding catch a glimpse of something mysterious and infinitely desirable and definitely *there.*

They might sing a hymn of the old-fashioned kind, in which you have to struggle with the syntax but the rhymes are so satisfactory, the puzzlement adds to the sum of the parts. All glory, laud and honour, and so forth.

They could pray for the sick—and as the list of names is read out, wonder about the lives they lived, and how no man is an island.

114

Some phrase they've heard from somewhere. Rachel could think how really she ought to go and visit her grandfather in an old persons' home, properly run and inspected, but lonely. They could repent of their sins, and giggle because obviously it was absurd to think of the elderly congregation, kneeling at the communion rail with ankle-less legs and wrinkled stockings, committing sins of fornication, let alone getting down to sweep up the crumbs under anyone's table. No-one today has sins. They have issues which need to be resolved. Same thing.

But for a fraction of a second Jacqui could remember how her nephews call her Auntie Bug Meanie, and resolve to do better.

They could listen to the choir for five minutes—a spot of polyphony in the sepulchral gloom. They could long to leave but not quite like to push their way through the lines of old folk. Already they're more moral creatures.

When they leave, Rachel and Jacqui will shiver a little and say, 'I don't want to die' and wonder briefly what happens after death. They are right to waste no time on it— nobody can possibly know. That in itself intrigues them. They're doing really well.

Exercise 4: Go See a Landscape

Jacqui and Rachel can take a coach from Victoria to a beauty spot within easy reach of London—hills and valleys, ripe for exultation, patchworked by the green fields of man's endeavour. There's nothing to *do*, though at least there's a stall where they can get a Diet Coke, and a fellow tourist says, 'Listen, is that a lark?' and they take out the plugs in their ears and forget to put them back. The wind in their ears is strange and interesting.

Or instead they could just go up to Hampstead Heath on the bus, after half an hour in Covent Garden, where you can buy lucky rose crystal rings at £15, and get off at the Kenwood entrance. Walk along past Kenwood House, and catch a glimpse of a Fragonard through the windows, and a note or two of Handel's 'Water Music' from the outdoor concert hall drifting through the air, and climb a hill or two amongst summer grasses and see the misty view over London, way over to the Surrey hills and the streaks of sunset red in the western sky.

Red sky at night, shepherd's delight.

'Does the sun always sink in the west?' asks Rachel.

'Duh!' says Jacqui. 'Everyone knows that.'

'Well, I don't,' says Rachel.

'I think it does move a few inches or something,' says Jacqui kindly, 'either way.'

Which shows you how she is improving. A month back she'd have hugged the idea of Rachel's ignorance to herself and rejoiced. A last gleam of sunlight strikes her black-rooted blonde head and looks for a moment almost like a halo.

I hope they did go up to Hampstead because on the way back in the bus they would then sit behind two students, one called Jude, doing design at Camberwell, and Ralph, studying marine biology at the Imperial Institute. Jacqui and Rachel fell into conversation about the Proms, Van Gogh's chair, the many-skirted girls of Fragonard, and Jacqui said, 'What was that thing about no man is an island?'

At which Jude turned round and quoted a John Donne poem he once learned by heart for an oral English exam. He stumbled a little but remembered most of it:

No man is an island, entire of itself,
Every man is a piece of the continent, a
  part of the main.
If a clod be washed away by the sea
Europe is the less, as well as if a
  promontory were,
As well as if a manor of thy friends or of
  thine own were.
Any man's death diminishes me, because I
  am involved in mankind,
And therefore never send to know for
  whom the bell tolls.
It tolls for thee.

After that, with their strengthened and well-exercised souls, they all got on like a house on fire, and though Jacqui felt enough loyalty to Corin to stay with him, Rachel eventually moved in with Jude.

I am not suggesting that a good man is necessarily the reward for virtue. On the other hand, there is nothing like an enthusiasm for the arts to help you leap class and educational boundaries.

The elevated soul calls to the elevated soul.

Family

Families make you happy.

   Your sister turning up at the door unexpectedly, bearing gifts.

   Your mother saying she's proud of you.

   Your father saying the same.

   Your brother lending you his car.

   Your grandmother—the happily married one—leaving you her wedding ring.

   Your children asleep, safe, sound and smiling.

   Your husband bringing you flowers.

   Your stepchild giving you a kiss.

That is, if you're a happy family to begin with.

If not, we can see quite another scenario:

   Your sister turns up. You pretend to be out.

Your mother and father say they're not going to pay back your student loan.

Your brother's car's a death trap. Is he doing it on purpose?

Your grandmother's putting a guilt trip on you: she wants you to get married.

You couldn't get a babysitter and you could be at a party. Why did you ever have children?

What's he trying to hide?

Little toad.

How did you get into this state? By spite, meanness, malice, carelessness, a general *'Why should I?'* and *'Who do you think you are?'* That's how.

You got into this state by flirting with your sister's partner, spending your student loan on drink and drugs, driving your brother's car for a week with the oil light on, telling your grandmother you've got chlamydia, habitually keeping the babysitter until dawn, being unfaithful yourself and pointing out to your stepchild that you're not her mother and never will be, when the child's real mother is an alcoholic.

You're not likely to do *all* these things, I agree, but just one or two is more than enough to make for very unsatisfactory family Christmases. I should make do with friends, if I were you. The family might be happier without you. Your 'making do' might be more like them 'putting up with'. You might even have to treat all your friends to Christmas lunch at some fancy hotel to make sure they turn up.

But you too can be loveable, if you would only change your ways. Remember that if you can't say anything nice, it's better to say nothing at all.

Remember that if you want to be happy you'd better be good.

The Instinctive Approach to Family Life

The Darwinians and neo-Darwinians take a stern, harsh, horrid view of family life. They see the child as using up the parents' resources of food, care and attention and when it's sucked them dry spitting them out and discarding them, leaving their poor depleted husks behind. As a sideline the child does its best to elbow its siblings right out of the nest— the more parental nourishment and attention that goes to them, the less left for it.

If the father has any sense, he's off too, before the growing son takes over as head bull and gores him to death. He may well have gone already, of course, to build another family, spread the selfish gene.

See instinct in unhappy action in the child who grows up and leaves home and never gets in touch again. It happens. Just a card at Christmas if you're lucky.

See innate sibling rivalry in the way the older child beats up the younger and the younger uses cunning to get the older into trouble.

It's there in all of us. In the least socialized of us, in whom the soul is least elevated, it's there the most.

If the culture tells you the life of the instinct is okay, it's easy to believe it. It suits us. *Do what thou wilt shall be the whole of the Law.* If the culture says it's every man, or woman, for themselves, that's the way it will very quickly be. So hell might quickly come to Earth.

Yet other forces are at work, too. Natural affection, given a chance, and when mixed with oughts and shoulds, is remarkably resilient.

See it on the train as Jacqui did, going home for Christmas—so many returning family members, so many gifts and ribbons and a kind of thrill in the air. Even those who most hate Christmas feel they ought to go home and do.

See how siblings love to reminisce, old feuds forgotten. Except at funerals, when they flare again. Who gets the oak table, who gets the silver cutlery, who got the most love and attention? Then the self-serving instinct subsides again, family affection reasserts itself, sibling speaks to sibling again and former wrongs are forgotten. This one stores the furniture, that one guarantees the rent—a mini-tribe within the tribe, that's the family.

So value it: subdue self-seeking instinct; bury the spitting, fighting, snarling aspect of family life. Don't remind your mother of the time she got drunk. Don't say to your child, *'If you can't remember what it was you said, it can't have been very important.'* It's mean and rejecting. Try blaming yourself, not them. Then the family will make you happy, not unhappy, because virtue is on your side. They will look to you and love you: you occupy the moral high ground. The bitchery and resentments will stop, the eating up of the soul in gripings, and brooding about wrongs done to you and vengeance planned by you.

And keep your motives clear. Think not, *'One day I might need them.'* Rather think, *'Today they need me.'*

Did you, reading that, think, *'Oh yuck!'* Did the gorge rise in your throat at such sentimentality? The *'yuck'* moment is when sentimentality (nature) and rationality (nurture) collide. The more educated you are, the more able nurture is to win over nature and the sooner you'll say *'Yuck.'*

For sentimentality is instinctive: the surge of emotion, the lump in the throat, is to do with the protection of the young and helpless. Any mammal with eyes which are large in proportion to the head causes the *'Aaah!'* reaction in any adult. Wolves will suckle human babies. Farmer's wives will spoonfeed lambs. Think kittens, think Audrey Hepburn, think Goldie Hawn. Starving children in Africa speak to us more than their starving mothers. We can't rest until they are fed.

If the sentimentality leads us to moral action, that's fine. Doing good, as we know, makes us happy. But for how long?

Let me tell you a parable about Jason, William and Zoë, three young people who thought they could save the world, their parents Doug and Gail, and Janet, who came along for the ride.

You might think the world is in such a state that it is beyond saving, but that is the voice of an older generation speaking. Take no notice.

The Joyous Multitude

Gail looked at her children across the breakfast table on Sunday morning and wondered how she and Douglas had done it. She had always considered herself rather dull, plain and dumpy, and Doug was frankly rather short, thin and gangly, with eyes too close together. She had married him in a fit of generosity to make up for his mother being so nasty to him and because her mother said looks in a man didn't matter. Yet between them they had produced three singularly attractive young people, Jason, William and Zoë, with cheerful dispositions, kindly natures, broad brows and wide-apart eyes, all granted by the grace of God the ability and desire to pass exams and at the moment all back from college, recovered from Glastonbury, recovering from Live 8 in London on the Saturday and intending to be at the G8 demo on the Monday. If the Toyota held out. Douglas would not let them take the Mercedes. Yet some of Gail and Doug's contemporaries, better looking and posher, had managed only dull, inward-looking and neurotic children, dropouts and drug addicts who were a perpetual shame and worry to their parents.

Luck of the draw, Gail supposed, and they'd been lucky.

At the moment, in between eating scrambled eggs and bacon, the young people were singing Sting's 'We'll Be Watching You' in chorus, and, what was more, in perfect harmony.

Douglas was opening the post. Whatever it was didn't please him.

'Hang on a bit,' said Gail. 'I thought it was "I'll Be Watching You", the stalker's anthem.'

'It's "we" now,' said Jason. 'Everything's changed since you were a girl. The people of the world have got their eye on the leaders of the world, that's what last night in Hyde Park was all about.'

'Sting was fabulous,' said William. 'Bush, Blair, Chirac—all the villains, named and shamed. The West can't get away with it any more.'

'I want to get to the shops to buy white clothes for Edinburgh tomorrow,' said Zoë. 'White bands aren't enough. It's Janet's fault. All my white T-shirts are grey. She put them in the wash with Jason's black Armani underpants. That girl is really and truly thick.'

Janet was 22, dyslexic, and helped Gail out sometimes in the house and garden.

'There were eight loads of washing after Glastonbury,' said Gail. 'Perhaps Janet just got fed up with sorting. You three couldn't be woken.'

'That's Glastonbury for you,' said Douglas. 'Mud and exhaustion. Thank God our water isn't metered. Yet.'

He put down the letter. It was from his accountant. It was not cheerful. His business was failing. Another twenty skilled staff would have to be laid off. The demand for British-made high-quality reusable medical instruments was falling. Since AIDS, mad cow disease and the prion scares—prions can survive even steam sterilization—more and more hospital equipment was required to be throwaway. And now China was entering the market in a big way. Meanwhile Zoë and the boys needed to be kitted out in white to save the whale or whatever it was this time. Their bracelets ran up their wrists like rainbows to their forearms. They were good children and he was proud of them. He had saved them from the harsh lessons of life and with any luck they need never learn them.

The doorbell rang. It was Janet. Her mother

was an alcoholic and her father a chronic depressive, but together they had produced a sweet, pretty, blonde girl who worked full time in a baker's shop, part time as a hairdresser and in her spare time for Gail. She was saving up for the deposit on a house and had been since she left school at 16. She spent nothing on herself if she could help it and had £23,000 in the post office.

Seeing the family was still having breakfast, Janet went straight out into the garden and started dead-heading roses and stripping the unsightly yellow rose leaves which had appeared overnight. The garden was to be opened to the public for the first time on Monday morning as part of the National Gardens Scheme. The gate takings were to go to the charity of Gail's choice. It was a great honour to be accepted onto the scheme. Gail had worked for fifteen years with this in mind, breaking stones and sifting earth, laying down lawns, planting trees and shrubs, and now her roses were the best in the neighbourhood. Never let it be said that just because she was a stay-at-home mother she didn't work hard. Janet had been helping Gail in the garden and house since she was 10.

'Janet is so embarrassing, Mum,' said Zoë. 'It isn't right to employ domestic staff. It's okay when she does the garden, but it feels unethical when she cleans up after us.'

Zoë liked Janet less than the boys did. Janet looked fragile, but wasn't. Zoë looked zippy and confident, but wasn't.

Janet came in for coffee. She told Gail she was having trouble with the sprinkler. The water pressure from the mains was so weak it was hardly enough to make it rotate. There was talk of a hosepipe ban in the area.

'That's nuts,' said William. 'It was raining most of last week. And you should have been at Glastonbury! The mud!'

'Yeah, I noticed,' said Janet. 'But here the ground's so hard the rain just runs off. And the water table's falling. It's the new estate up on the hill. Eight hundred new houses.'

'A hosepipe ban!' shuddered Gail. 'I might as well just give up on the garden. Those dreadful little houses!'

'Don't be such a snob, Mum,' said Jason.

'You're such Nimbys, you two,' said Zoë.

'Nimbys?' asked Douglas,

'Not in my back yard,' explained William.

Doug refrained from saying it was all very well for them, they were away at college a lot of the time, or in bed, or at festivals, or concerts, or parties. They didn't notice how busy the roads had become, or how crowded the trains, and how with the coming of the supermarket all the small shops had closed.

William was now explaining to Janet about the Make Poverty History concert and why it was important. How noble Bob Geldof was going to Make Poverty History, and how all the good people were going along to the G8 summit in Edinburgh to make sure world leaders noticed.

'I've never been to a concert,' said Janet. 'Why, when you can download the stuff for free? I've never been to a demo either.'

'A protest virgin,' said William appreciatively.

'But I'd quite like to go one day,' said Janet. 'Just to see what it's like. It might be exciting.'

'Why don't you come to Edinburgh with us this evening?' asked William. 'There's a spare seat in the car.'

Zoë gestured *no, no*. She hated travelling in crowded cars and Janet would be a drag. But William and Jason didn't seem to notice.

Douglas opened the letter he had left until last. It was from the Inland Revenue. It said his appeal had been turned down; the disputed £37,000 was indeed owed. He had hoped to get the children through college without student loans, so they didn't have to start their lives loaded with debt. He could forget that.

'We'll be dangerously squashed,' said Zoë. 'Unless of course Dad lets us take the Mercedes. Did you know that for every extra student in a car the accident rate rises exponentially?'

'Perhaps you'd better,' said Douglas. The clapped-out Toyota was a safety risk; the M1 horrendous. The word 'squashed' brought horrific headlines to mind: 'Protesters in motorway mayhem horror.' He'd had too much bad news lately. You got to expect more.

'But they're depending on me at the baker's,' said Janet. 'We're short-staffed.'

'Saving the world is more important,' said Jason, 'than serving the already overfed with cakes and buns. You know how many children die every in Africa from starvation? One a second!'

Click, click, click, they went with their fingers.

'One click, one death,' said Zoë.

'That's awful,' said Janet. 'I'll come.'

The M1 was busy. Old bangers, coaches, all converging on Edinburgh. Everyone dressed in white. Jason driving, Zoë in the passenger seat, William and Janet in the back. Make Poverty History. So much goodwill! Of course it would happen.

'Isn't it exciting?' said William. His hand was on Janet's slender knee. Any minute he'd put her arm round her. It wasn't going far, because she worked in the local baker's and aspired to nothing and he was taking a philosophy degree, but you never knew.

Janet thought William was a bit of a twat, like the rest of his family, but she liked his fingers. They felt quite electric.

'I don't know anything about politics,' she said. 'I've never taken an interest. You'll have to tell me.'

They told her.

'Those G8 leaders must be real scumbags,' said Janet, horrified. 'Starving all those poor little African children!'

'They don't want to share,' said Jason. 'They want all the wealth for themselves.'

'But if we give more to Africa, does it mean we'll have to pay more tax?' asked Janet.

'The West can afford it,' said Zoë.

'I can't,' said Janet. 'You should see my pay slips as it is! And I don't know how long my job is going to last. Krispy Creme Donuts are opening down the road.'

There was slightly awkward silence. Then they tried to explain about debt relief and free trade, but it wasn't much use.

'I'd be ashamed to have debts,' said Janet. 'I was brought up to pay my own way.'

She was very difficult. Jason and Zoë wished they hadn't brought her along, but William was holding her hand.

They talked about Bush's satanic empire, about the illegitimacy of the Iraq War and the problem of obesity, which was not theirs.

An old banger passed them at dangerous speed, its many occupants making slitty throat gestures.

'Just being in a Mercedes,' said Zoë crossly, 'doesn't mean we're rich.'

A coach passed. The passengers were draped in white, with white face masks and black holes for eyes.

'Like the Ku Klux Klan,' said Janet. 'Spooky.'

'I'll look after you,' said William.

'I still don't understand why it's our fault the Iraqis are blowing themselves up,' Janet complained.

'Bush started it off,' explained Jason patiently. 'He destabilized the region. He should have left well alone. It wasn't democracy he was after, it was oil.'

Douglas had filled the tank for them before they left, which was just as well, there were such queues at the petrol stations.

'You mean Saddam Hussein was a good thing?' Janet sounded surprised. 'My dad said he cut out people's tongues if he didn't like what they said. And that's what he'd do to me if I didn't shut up.'

William gently disengaged his hand from Janet's. What was he getting into? Her home life sounded a bit strong for him. Sorry for her and all that, and it must be hell to be dyslexic, but even so.

'My mum likes Tony Blair,' Janet continued. 'She says the government's doing all right. She gets free detox sessions.'

'Tony Blair!' the others shrieked. 'Bush's poodle! All those refugees sent back to Zimbabwe, back to torture and death!'

'But we can't keep everyone,' said Janet. 'The whole of Zimbabwe would be over here if they could. Who'd want to live there when they could live here?'

They were in a traffic jam now, cars from all over the country converging on Edinburgh. Flags, banners, laughing, singing, everyone of one mind—fabulous. In the free car park the sounds of Pink Floyd, Sting and Madonna came floating through the crisp early morning air, warring for precedence.

'I bet that concert was just a money-making scam, nothing to do with Make Poverty History at all,' said Janet.

They were sorry they'd brought her.

'And I expect that's what all this Geldof stuff

is really about too,' she went on. 'If we make Africa a better place to live in they won't want to come over here. It's just all one big conspiracy, isn't it, the way you say.'

Too horrified for words, they managed to lose her when the march was forming. They didn't feel good about it, but how could you communicate with someone so stupid?

They marched in the slowly winding procession up towards the castle. Make Poverty History! It was hard to see how the world would not be saved with so much hard work, organization and goodwill all focused here.

Round about teatime William worried a little about losing Janet. Would she be okay?

'The Janets of the world will always survive,' said Zoë. But even as she spoke her mobile buzzed and fluttered in her pocket.

It was Janet. She was in the infirmary. She'd got caught up in a riot of some kind. The doctors were keeping her in overnight and possibly longer. She had concussion and they didn't want her brain to swell.

'But she hasn't got a brain *to* swell,' said Zoë, and the others giggled before they shushed her for her wickedness. She didn't think Janet had heard.

It was a great nuisance. They couldn't just leave her. They'd have to go and check her injuries out.

A&E was crowded with casualties from the march. There had been some trouble—not much, they were told, but of course Janet had managed to get caught up with the anarchists and on the wrong side of the riot police. She was a bit battered around the head and had a nasty black eye. They were keeping her in for observation, but there was no need to worry.

Jason, William and Zoë agreed they couldn't wait for her, they had a party tomorrow. Janet said it was okay, she'd just take the train back once she was discharged. But then she complained about having to spend money on the fare home, which was a bit much—everyone knew she had £23,000 in the bank.

When Jason, William and Zoë got back home on the Tuesday night their mother was in tears on the lawn. The water pressure had finally fallen so low the sprinklers had stopped rotating and there'd been no one to put up the *'Open to the Public'* signs. She'd only had thirteen visitors, after all of those years making the desert bloom.

'But what's the matter?' they asked her.

'Nothing, darlings,' she said, as was her wont. 'Nothing important.'

On the Thursday the bombs went off in London and all Gail thought mattered was that her children were safely home.

Moral

We could try charity begins at home. Never were there three more self-centred, self-righteous and bigoted young persons than Jason, William and Zoë. Selfish too. Mud at Glastonbury is a joyous thing so long as there is someone else to clear it up. They never lift a finger to help their mother in the garden. It never crosses their mind that their father has business worries. They spend all their energy being good.

But they are happy. And by many people's standards they are really quite good. They are at least trying. When it comes to charity, though they may see 'home' as starting far away, in distant places, they shake boxes, go on marches and do their best, so long as it does not inconvenience them too much. None of them will stay with Janet; she does not agree with them and it is easy to dismiss her as stupid. And no one they know takes any notice of concussion.

You could also quarrel with Jason, William and Zoë because they look past the beggar outside their new supermarket, not meeting his eye, though noticing that his dog looked well fed enough, and reproach their father when he gave voice to his marvel that Social Services gave extra money to claimants with pets, out of his taxes.

'You are such a right-wing fascist, Daddy,' Zoë often complains, while he signs the cheque, and when her mother murmured once, of the beggar, 'I hope he spends all that money on bones, not drugs,' she pouted about the house for hours, saying her mother was drug phobic, and it was dangerous to give dogs bones, anyway, they could splinter.

But she loves her mother and her mother loves her. They are a happy family. It is too easy to be irritated when it comes to other people's happiness, and we should not succumb to the feeling. We must give them credit where credit is due, and remember that young people do learn.

This lot will have to. Douglas is to go bankrupt, and the house to be sold by Inland

Revenue at a knock-down price.

Fortunately Gail has a little money of her own and they end up living in a pretty cottage in Ireland, in a lush spot with a high rainfall. Her garden wins prizes locally. The children visit frequently. Jason becomes an estate agent, selling rural plots for business development, William has given up philosophy and is a banker, and Zoë, who always did have too much of a liking for drugs, took up with a Rastafarian and has two children and no money.

Janet did not have concussion but lost her job. The baker's did close. But she married the manager of Krispy Creme and sits on the Town Council where her contribution is most valued. She has a keen eye for waste, and expenditure has been cut to the bone. She taks about her visit to Edinburgh when she was a girl as a real eye-opener.

And really, actually, all of them except Janet could be described as happy. That's what comes of having a loving family.

Shopping

We gather in stores, in the good times, to keep ourselves going through the hard times. (That's a pun. Gather in stores of grain in the cave. Gather in stores to shop together, in the new world. See?)

We do it with food. Our bodies lay down fat in order for us to feed from it in times of scarcity. Think of the brown bear, plump as can be after a good autumn, but skinny as a rake when the thaw comes and she emerges, skin hanging in folds, from hibernation.

The Atkins diet works by tricking the body into believing it's starving, that it's got to break down fat if it's going to survive.

It's just a pity the times of scarcity never come. Strawberries were a once-a-year treat. Now they're always growing somewhere in the world—just snap your fingers and they're there. *How about some caster sugar? And lashings of cream?'*

We like to have the cave nicely filled with *things*. In case we run out. A hefty pile of moss to put the baby on. An extra bearskin. Wood for the fire. *Gather in, preserve, save, collect.*

Of course we shop. Always have. Or bartered. Your nose bone for my beads.

It's instinct, at it again. The urge to ornament the self. To get yourself a super man. He brings the meat back, though you gather the berries. *'That's a pretty red! Let's have it!'* Excavations of prehistoric peoples always turn up some female ornament or other.

Socialization brings us the credit card, the bank account, the bargain offer. How can we resist? Some men like us to spend. *'My wife, she shops till she drops!'* Proud.

The alpha male deserves the alpha female. The brave deserve the fair. So don't beat yourself up about this either. The urge to acquire is in your genes. Acquisition. It's Mother Nature at her fiendish work again.

Just remember, twelve pairs of shoes are fine, but twenty-four are pushing it. Twelve are forgivable, twenty-four or more are bad, an offence against the sumptuary laws. Sell surplus shoes on eBay and give to charity. You're never going to wear them and only a few of them will fit.

Shopping? Just Do It!

I have a bright-blue and yellow mug which carries the slogan *'Shopping? Just do it!'* It is my favourite mug. On it is a giddy-looking and totally happy girl, of the garage pin-up kind.

Happy, yes, but for how long? What happens next? *Bills.* Shopping is a source of great pleasure and also, naturally, a source of female guilt and anxiety.

If a woman has children there's no end to it. *'Now how am I going to buy their clothes? I've signed up for this new car and what about their maths tutoring? They will never pass their exams and it will all be my fault!'*

If she hasn't got children it's not much better. *'Why on earth did I buy that? It's the wrong colour/too large/too small/too cheap/too dear for what I wanted. There's no space left in the wardrobe as it is. If I saved instead of spent I could buy a house or get a pension.'*

And on the way home on the bus, the seat next to you piled with bags in shiny white and pink, bursting out with folds of white tissue, or the soft cloth of a shoebag, your breath starts coming in short gasps. A fully fledged anxiety attack: sweats, trembles and all. And no amount of breathing into a brown paper bag as recommended (first find one!) will stop it. Anxiety has struck and it's not even free-floating—it is specific to shopping. (More about free-floating anxiety later.)

You could step off the bus and leave the bags behind, and with it the evidence of your guilt—it's not as if you actually needed anything you bought—but it would be an even worse waste of money. You could sell the stuff on eBay. Yes, that makes you feel better.

The normal advice—*'If it makes you feel guilty, don't do it'*—doesn't seem quite to apply. Stopping it would make you extremely unhappy. And who wants to drink from a mug that says, *'Shopping? Don't do it!'* Not me.

Your writer was brought up in a poverty-stricken household. She's never quite got over it. Schoolfriends would look in shop windows, say, *'I rather like that,'* and just go in and buy whatever it was. It seemed an infinitely desirable kind of life and she assumed it would never be hers. She was accustomed to averting her eyes when passing a shop window in case she was overwhelmed with longing for something she couldn't have.

Yet in the end she too could say, *'I like that, I'll take it'* or *'Let's go by taxi, it's quicker'* or

144

even *'Let's hire a car with a driver, it's so much less effort.'* Now she is simply not good any more at frugality, and not inclined to wish it on others.

All I'm going to say for once is if you want to shop, shop. Shop some more. Put up with the boring details of what comes later. Debt, ruin, misery. Shopping? Just do it!

(I all but bought a pair of Roman earrings once, a bunch of purple grapes in a gold setting. I didn't buy them. I had a feeling they might be 'funerary objects' and had been found in some tomb. Then I changed my mind. I just wanted them. When I went back to the shop they had gone. I have lamented them ever since, and that was eight years ago. You know how it is? When it comes to shopping those who hesitate are lost.)

Driven to Ruin

Emma, in Flaubert's novel *Madame Bovary*, was driven to suicide by her passion for shopping. It wasn't disclosure to her husband of her many affairs which did it, it wasn't the sheer boredom of his presence, it was because, my feeling always was, she brought ruination on him by buying pretty things. She offered to sell her pretty proud self to the shopkeeper to whom she owed all the money—M. Hereux, but he pushed her aside. He didn't want her, he wanted his money. He'd encouraged her to run up debts. He despised her.

And when the crunch came, her lovers declined to help her. They were married now, they had other commitments, it was inconvenient. Love's love and then it's over! And she had so believed and trusted it was for ever, that it was a sacred thing. In love! And things, the pretty things, the silly things that you find in shop windows, were her ruination. Money is real, love is not.

She bought silk embroidered slippers for one lover, a silver case for another and little gifts for her husband. She bought pretty clothes for her daughter and lit the candles every day, not just on formal occasions. Her mother-in-law knew it would all end it tears, but her husband adored her and couldn't bear to stop her. She bought a new cloak lined with silk to run away in and a new studded trunk to take with her. But the lover she was absconding with didn't turn up. Perhaps because she'd warned him in passing that the daughter was coming too. And Emma went on spending, and the interest kept rising. She forged her husband's signature and in the end there was no way the family could be saved. She took her life, but her husband was ruined anyway.

Mind you, the story was written by a man. I think if it had been written by a woman Emma would have got away with it. One of the lovers would have turned up trumps. An admirer would have left her a fortune. Something. She would have lived happily ever after, lover after lover, and her husband would never have found out. That's much more like real life. And who is to say, as she grew older, being happy, she might have been good, and being good, she might have been happy—if only for lack of opportunity.

Shopping with the Hungry

Let me tell you my experience of going shopping with four Hollywood wives. They were all as skinny as rakes and as glamorous as hell. (Your writer has other things to think about than her appearance, and it shows, but they were good enough to take me out window shopping and endure the embarrassment.)

'Not shopping?' I asked, disappointed.

'Just window shopping,' they said firmly.

We trooped along an avenue in Century City.

It was lined with restaurants, confectioners, delicatessens, cheese and chocolate shops, interspersed with stores selling Bach remedies, crystals, healing essences and so forth, as if the latter somehow neutralized the former, absolved you of the sin of being fat.

The wives' limbs were thin and sun-bedded, their manicures bright, their clothes in many tones of beige. Their gold jewellery clanked. I stomped around in flat shoes for wide feet; they wore Manolos even to shop.

We looked in windows. We studied the cream cakes, the mammoth Easter eggs, the little tins of caviare, so exquisitely expensive. As we walked, and loitered, and loitered and walked, we discussed, in principle, without of course tasting, the difference between Belgian chocolates and Manhattan chocolates, the merits of Italian garlic salami as opposed to French and whether maraschino cherries should be described as bitter or sweet. We talked only about food.

The wives seemed to have total recall of every morsel they had ever tasted. They recalled but did not eat. They found their pleasure where they could, enjoying the view from the dietary moral high ground. Elbowing others off with their thin, sharp elbows.

They came to a café which seemed familiar to them. It was midday. Their jewels were glittering, their chins were stretched, their eyes were wide.

'Shall we go in for just a cup of coffee?' asked one nervously.

They seemed to ponder.

'Black coffee,' said another.

'Of course black,' they chorused. But it was obvious that the one who had first suggested coffee was the weakest and had lost status.

We all went in and had black coffee. Around us men were eating heartily. The aroma of roasting chicken assailed us.

'I think I'm just going to have a salad,' said the one who'd first suggested coffee. Well, what did she have to lose? She was bottom of the pile.

'Without dressing,' she added.

The salad came. Everyone stared at it. She ate it, leaf by miserable leaf.

'Tell you what,' she said, 'I'm going to have a piece of chocolate cake.'

149

'Chocolate cake,' she said to the waiter, and he instantly brought out a great square of cream-filled chocolate cake which practically filled the table and four plates and spoons and handed them round.

The wives all ate voraciously until there wasn't a scrap left. I didn't need to. I'd had breakfast.

'Happens all the time,' said the waiter to me, as we left. 'I know that sort by heart. I save them the embarrassment of asking.'

It just goes to show, challenge instinct too much and instinct fights back and wins. Train youself to relish hunger, which dieters should do, but even so it's hard. The body fights back. The appetites of the flesh are huge and those of the spirit can get a little attenuated.

Use one instinct to control another. Play off the instinct to acquire against the instinct to eat. We should have stopped off at Tiffany's and bought some jewellery.

This is the parable of Emily and how she achieved happiness by falling in love and not going shopping.

Nothing to Wear

It was at half-past four on Tuesday, 6 June that Charles realized he had a problem. He and Emily had plans for the evening. They were to have tea at the Ritz—he'd booked it for five—and after that they were to go on to the summer exhibition at Burlington House. They have been invited to a private view.

Tea at the Ritz was mostly for Charles, for when he visited his old mother in her care home on Sunday afternoon and gave an account of his week. Tea at the Ritz was a useful talking-point, being a concept the old lady could still understand, and there were allied subjects to discuss, such as how no one knew how to make cucumber sandwiches any more, let alone how to blanch cucumber. And Emily quite liked the Ritz. She said she found it relaxing.

Then they'd go on to Burlington House across the road and if they got there early, Charles might well meet up with his friend Marlowe. Then he could casually mention the good studio property about to come on the market in South Ken., a snip at two and a half million. He knew Marlowe was looking. If it worked, there'd be a good commission in it for Charles.

But it was already half past four and here was Emily not even dressed and not quite sitting but somehow crouched, folded on the bedroom carpet, wailing, 'I've nothing to wear.'

She crouched in her silk slip, pretty as a picture by a slightly astigmatic painter, her legs so long and her hips so slim—backèd like a swan, as the folk song had it—that for the first time it struck Charles that there was something unreasonable about her looks. Other girls were pear-shaped, or had short necks, and complained of not being able to find clothes to fit. But Emily was the one designers liked to lend clothes to for grand occasions, because she showed them off so well. She catwalk modelled sometimes, when she could be bothered, which was not often. She gave the impression of having sprung to life not from between human thighs but from a sketch in some couturier's notebook. Yet her mother was dumpy enough.

I've nothing to wear,' she repeated, 'not a thing.'

They had been married for five months and Charles realized by now that Emily had dressing problems the way other girls had eating problems, but he loved her and he indulged her, or at any rate had until now, when he suddenly found himself irritated. She sat surrounded by Blahnik shoes, and Ferreti dresses, and Etro jackets, and leather skirts by Versace, and Westwood corsets, torn from their hangers and flung anywhere on the floor, and the price of them added up was beyond belief. His pocket was not bottomless: he had to wheel and deal like anyone else, and it was not easy.

'I don't want us to be late,' he said rashly. 'Just put on any old thing. You always look fantastic.'

'Men always say that,' she said. 'It isn't true. I look absurd. For one thing my head is too small for my body. Haven't you even noticed?'

'I think it's about the same as anyone else's,' he said, but he could see what she meant. She went to the gym every morning: exercise developed her shoulders but not her head, so she did seem a little out of proportion.

'I'm a monster,' she said. 'A freak. My eyes look like that alien's in *ET.*'

'You could eat more,' he suggested and she threw a boot at him and laughed. He loved her laugh. 'Seriously, though,' she said, 'I haven't a thing to wear.'

He picked up a filmy silk thing without much top. 'How about this? It's a nice colour.'

'Don't be absurd,' she said. 'It might work for the summer exhibition, but then there's tea at the Ritz as well.'

He could see that it had become his fault that she had nothing to wear, because of his mother.

'People will be looking at their sandwiches and the paintings, not at you,' he said, though it wasn't true and he knew it. He didn't want to miss Marlowe. It would be difficult enough finding him in the crush.

'That thing you wore to Ascot,' he suggested.

'That's the whole *point*, I wore it to Ascot. And it's no good without a hat anyway. And nobody who isn't weird or my mother wears a hat to an art show.'

'I just wear a suit,' he said, 'and it could be any old suit.'

'That's simply not true. I married an Armani man. Don't go and change on me!'

Her wardrobe took up the whole wall. Scarcely a day went by without her buying something new. Sometimes she just shoved the bags at the back of the cupboard to open later and forgot all about them.

'I've nothing to wear,' she said again.

'You're turning into a weirdo,' he said, losing patience. 'Just put something on and hurry up about it. I'll order a taxi now.'

Tears welled up in the enormous eyes and rolled down her thin cheeks. She was not accustomed to harsh words. He felt bad and after he'd ordered the taxi he sat on the floor with her to be companionable.

'But I'm not being unreasonable,' she said, snuggling into him. 'It's just the shoes are doing my head in. I'm going to have to walk from the Ritz to Burlington House and you can never sit down at private views, and supposing my feet begin to hurt? If the rest is right the shoes aren't and vice versa. And Genia Marlowe will be there and Marlowe's made her pregnant and she'll stand there with her six-month bump in stretch Versace being mobbed by the media. Babies are chic, but personally I think she looks totally yuck.'

'Look,' Charles said, 'if you want a baby I'm not all that set against it.' He had been married before and had two almost grown-up children and was well into his forties. Emily was not yet 30.

'Are you crazy? What makes you think I want to have a baby?'

'But you said you did,' he said, taken by surprise.

'Did I? That must have been a long time ago, before we were married. I've changed my mind. Genia Marlowe says she's going to breastfeed. I think that is so completely disgusting.'

'The taxi's here,' he said.

She uttered a shriek, stretched her long limbs out on the carpet and thrummed her pretty little fists into the white pile. She was a having a tantrum.

Charles hadn't seen this before. He was afraid she would damage her feet as they banged against the floor.

He called up her mother in the country to ask for help. He'd never done that before either.

'Oh dear,' said Mrs Julia Forrester. 'Not again! She used to do that all the time when she was little. The church bell would be ringing for morning service and there'd be our little Emily, throwing a tantrum because her ankle socks had frills, or didn't, I can't remember which.'

Julia and her husband had recently downsized, perforce, and the big house was gone and now Julia grew roses in her cottage garden, and her husband read all the books he'd never had time to read when he was something in the City. They seemed happy enough. Emily's income fortunately came from a trust fund, but the expected inheritance would never come, which made it all the more important that Charles got to drop a word in Marlowe's ear.

'Perhaps it's because she's a younger sister,' Julia offered. 'She never quite thinks she has enough, and what she does have will never quite do. Or perhaps it's me. I've never wanted to wear anything other than a comfy jersey and an old skirt. I never liked being noticed and I never cared what others thought. I expect Emily likes to make up for what she sees as my shortcomings.' There was a tinge of acid in her voice.

'But what do I do with her?' asked Charles. 'I hate being late for things.'

'You're just like her father,' said Julia, 'a

stickler for punctuality. I expect that's why she married you. Now Katherine takes after me. Very relaxed. Sit it out is my advice and she'll be good as gold for the rest of the day. That's what I used to do.'

Charles called Katherine. Emily was still in her slip and still thrumming and outside the front door of the pretty little Chelsea house the taxi meter was clicking up.

Katherine was older than Emily by two years. She favoured a neater and more expensive version of her mother's clothes and changed their style only as Marks and Spencer did. She was married to a barrister and had three children. She went to Ascot not to be seen but to look at the horses and meet up with her sister. They were quite affectionate with one another.

'Get her to talk to me,' she said.

Emily consented to take the phone. She'd calmed down, though still gulped air. Charles listened from the other side of the door.

'It's Charles's fault,' complained Emily. 'He's so weird. He only wants to go to the Ritz because of his dotty old mother, and I'm the living sacrifice, and he expects me to wear the same thing to both of them, and I've nothing to wear anyway.'

There was pause while Katherine spoke.

'That spotted la Croix thing? Are you joking? It's head to toe and last year's, and makes my bum look large, and nobody's wearing spots, and I have to show some flesh,' said Emily. 'Everyone will be showing flesh. Genia Marlowe will have a naked belly, I bet, with the navel pierced, if she can find it to pierce.'

Again Katherine spoke.

'Suede's cruel,' said Emily, 'you really are weird, Katherine. And it's far too solid, not in the least floaty, and floaty is in. I know you wear the same T-shirt three days running, but you live in the country where nobody sees you except kids and animals.'

Charles gave up and was about to send the taxi away when Emily came dancing out of the house wearing a pair of jeans, a lilac beaded chiffon blouse with frills and pointy gold shoes cut so low they showed her toes and so insubstantial he didn't see how they could carry all six feet of her. The secret no doubt lay in their cost. Her eyes were a little pink and she sniffed, but she leant up against him trustingly in the taxi. At the Ritz she ate a whole plateful of tiny cucumber sandwiches and looked so lovely, fresh and happy that people stared and there was an incident when a Japanese guest tried to take a photograph of her and security appeared out of nowhere and confiscated the camera.

'I must tell Genia Marlowe about that,' said Emily. She had been to school with Genia.

They crossed the road to Burlington House. Emily stepped into the bus lane without looking and Charles had to pull her back or she would have been run down.

'It was coming from the wrong direction!' complained Emily.

'You should have read the signs,' said Charles. 'It wasn't the driver's fault, it was yours.'

'Why do you always take my enemy's side?' she cried. 'You're so like my father I can't bear it.' She looked at him for a moment almost as if she hated him, but quickly composed her face again and took his arm. She limped a little but denied that it was anything to do with the shoes.

They arrived at the private view half an hour later than Charles had hoped and the

Marlowes had been and gone. There was a painting on the wall of a naked Genia, however, proudly pregnant. Journalists crowded round it and guests mobbed the painter, a burly, bearded young man in a tattered green jumper which looked as if he had slept in it. Certainly he had spilled soup down it.

Charles caught a glimpse of Tattery Abel the art dealer, a man reputed to be rich as Croesus, with four Edward Hoppers, three Jackson Pollocks and five Warhols to his name and who liked to dabble in painting himself. Failing Marlowe, he fell into conversation with Tattery and mentioned the fact that one of the best of the original studio houses in South Ken was coming onto the market soon, at about three mill. Tattery was undoubtedly interested and took Charles' e-mail address.

Charles looked for Emily and found her deep in conversation with the painter in the green jumper, while photographers from the gossip columns and the arts pages snapped away. She'd like that. No one seemed to take pictures of Charles any more, not since he'd taken a wife and stopped being the most eligible bachelor in town, even though it was Emily he had married. He wandered off to look at the paintings on the wall. He imagined Emily was persuading the artist to paint her portrait, and didn't doubt that she'd succeed.

Fifteen minutes later he came back to see how she was doing and found her sitting on a little gold chair while Green Jumper, on his knees, took off her shoes for her and put one in each pocket of his trousers, little heels sticking out. The artist helped her up, tucking her arm under his, and took off his sandals to keep her company, showing dirty toes, and the pair of them went round happily in bare feet, he deriding the paintings and Emily enthusing.

When next he went to look for Emily he couldn't find her. Fortunately, Marlowe turned up just then and said he'd seen her leaving with a weird-looking slob in a green jumper. They'd called a taxi. Charles mentioned the studio house in South Ken and was gratified by Marlowe's eager response. Now he could play Tattery off against Marlowe and the price would go up. He went home on his own.

The next time he saw Emily was when she opened the door to him a year later. She was living with Green Jumper in a dilapidated barn conversion in Essex. There had not been much to discuss in relation to the divorce; she'd left it all to his lawyers. Charles had claimed alimony and Emily hadn't argued, to the extent of leaving herself with barely enough to live on. She hadn't bothered to come back to collect her clothes.

Green Jumper hovered in the background while Charles got Emily to sign a few necessary documents. Charles stayed on the step and was not asked in. The house smelled of garlic, oil paint, dogs and turpentine. Emily was wearing a frumpy jumper like her mother's and a soiled suede skirt of an unflattering length, and she was pregnant.

If you had hardly anything at all to wear, he could see, having nothing to wear wouldn't matter too much, and the pain of it would be greatly eased. He was happy for her.

Parable ends.

And that is all I have to say on the subject of shopping.

Chocolate

'Time for myself, time for *me*,' is the desolate call of the new woman in a new age. Nurture overtakes nature. Her instincts have nowhere to go. Without the tribe she is desolate.

The birth rate falls, men become an optional extra, and love is neurotic dependency. Sex loses its savour. *'Because I deserve it, because I'm worth it!'* begins to sound hollow. Oh, hand me the chocolate bar, it's all I have left.

Six women out of ten, according to research, prefer chocolate to sex.

Can this be true?

An exhausted woman of 35 with three children and a career and a new baby in her arms might well prefer chocolate to what feels like male mauling—choose the soft melting of the sensuous stuff in the mouth to the demands of another's flesh.

A girl who is unhappy because her boyfriend has betrayed her and who never wants to have another man in her life might well claim to prefer chocolate to sex. Though experience suggests she will not feel like this for long.

A woman bored by the same sex with the same man in the same bed for too long a time might well prefer chocolate. But the situation is not likely to go on for long in modern society. One or the other will split. Probably him.

He: 'What's the matter? Do you have a headache?'

She: 'I'm just going down to the fridge to get some chocolate.'

And he thinks about the girl in the salsa class. He tried to give her a box of chocolates and she looked at him as if he were mad. But he likes a certain hauteur, a certain disdain, in a girl. And she's as slim as a whippet.

I am not saying that to frighten you. No woman should ever alter her actions because she is nervous that her husband fancies someone else. She should go to the fridge and come back to bed and eat the chocolate, under his nose, and offer him some, and then resume her love-making. She must appear indifferent to the interest he takes in other women. She must appear to take it as a compliment that though he says, *'Whoaar, look at that!'* when a pretty woman passes by, he remains with her. It would be very odd if men did not fancy other women, since they are creatures of nature as well as nurture. Nurture tells him it's bad manners, nature makes him spontaneous in his reactions. When he's not allowing himself to say *'Whoaar'* that's the time she should worry. He may be trying too hard.

Mind you, the craving for chocolate that affects so many women is hard to explain in Darwinian terms. It seems an entirely learned response. It is equally hard to explain in spiritual terms. Hard to imagine the Intelligent Designer perceiving his creation and saying, *'I know, the way to get this race to make moral choices is to create chocolate.'*

Mother love, male aggression, greed—all the kinds of things that play a part in the survival of the species and its better ability to glorify its creator, take part in the cosmic struggle between good and evil—all that, yes. But chocolate? Hardly.

Addictive, though. Chocolate, as most of us know by now, contains many of the substances which keep us happy and tranquil—the endorphins, serotonin, and so forth—though you'd have to take 240 lb of the stuff to get the effect of one marijuana reefer. That's why it's become traditional to give chocolate on Valentine's Day. (Though personally I think this is more to with the

Chocolate Council and the card industry than tradition. My generation had never heard of it, any more than they had of Mother's Day.) So you eat it because you like it, because it's sold to you by skilful brainwashing and advertising, because you shouldn't, because you want to spoil your dinner, because life around you seems vaguely unsatisfactory, because *it's there*. And life has spited you in some way and so you deserve a little treat.

Well, perhaps you do.

Chocolate comes under the heading of little treats, of whatever gets you through the night, of feast days and holidays and on the seventh day thou shalt rest and do no labour, of trinkets and bangles and new lipsticks, new face cream, new nail polish—little exercises in hope and betterment, the very pleasure of frittering away what should be saved. The denial of prudence. Delinquency.

Delinquency may be what pushes the tribe forward to better things. A refusal to accept things as they are. Boredom with the status quo. *'Let's do it this way, not that.'* And so we end up with carts, trains, cars, aircraft, television, space travel, nuclear fission, modern warfare, wind farms and boxes of chocolate.

Eat, eat and be damned to them!

Whatever gets you through the night. And that's enough about chocolate.

To cheer us up, let's have the parable of Marigold, who, finding herself in an unfamiliar tribe, took delight in upsetting its rituals. The tribe, of course, exacted punishment. She was lucky to escape with her life. But she did learn.

A Solitary Person

I am by nature a solitary person. If I were to advertise in a newspaper for a partner—and who hasn't at one time or another been tempted?—the entry would go something like this: *'Reclusive blonde young woman (32), workaholic, sharp-tongued, hates company, children, loud music, country walks, wining and dining, likes crosswords, seeks similarly inclined male. No smokers, no Viagra users.'* Nevertheless, when Marigold asked me to Badger House for the Christmas weekend I was glad of the invitation. Around Christmas, aloneness, that normally enviable and superior state, can feel suspiciously like loneliness.

'You don't have to talk to anyone,' said Marigold. 'You can sit in a dark corner amongst the pine needles and wrapping paper and pretend to be the *au pair*. My family won't even notice you, I promise.'

'Well,' I thought, 'don't be too sure of that. I can make people notice me if I put myself out.'

I share an office with Marigold. Fortunately she, like me, is a silent person. We are both the offspring of noisy ducal families who, having taken to drugs in the sixties, dropped babies like flies and failed to make proper arrangements for their upbringing beyond sending them off to boarding schools. Now, for both of us, just to be in a quiet room alone is bliss. I, for one, seek it perpetually. In the same way, my mother says, those children who were kept short of butter in World War II grew up to slather it on their bread for ever. Thus she excuses her own obesity.

My mother decamped with a movie-maker to California some four years ago and one by one my younger siblings drifted after her—I was the oldest of five. I could have gone out to join this new ersatz family of mine for the festive season, but I declined. I mention this so you don't feel sorry for me or see me as the kind of person who is short of places to go to at Christmas. It's just that I sometimes fail to want to go wherever it is in time and then end up miserable. But I do like to feel I have removed myself from company, not that company has removed itself from me.

I also need, I think, to point out to you that the benefits of my temperament are such that my confinement in this prison cell is not in itself onerous. Don't feel pity for me on this account. I have faith in justice and assume that I will be found innocent of a murder I did not commit, and in the meantime I rejoice that I won't be expected to go to some party to see in the New Year. I understand that here in Holloway we just all sit silently and separately in our cells on the dreaded night and contemplate the past and the future. Suits me.

No, indeed, sir, I did not murder Lady Hester Walpole Delingro. Let me tell my story in my own way, as is normally done, from the beginning. Or are you in some great hurry? Perhaps you Legal Aid solicitors are on piece-work? No? When I hear from my mother she'll have the best lawyers in town take over my case; it's just that she's staying oddly silent, so you will have to put up with me for the time being.

Badger House! My heart sank on seeing the place, at the wrong end of a two-hour standing journey on a crowded train which smelled of alcohol and mince pies. Marigold had showed me photographs of her family home. It looked lovely enough in the summer, with rampant nature creeping up to its door, but in midwinter, standing isolated and denuded of foliage, you could see it all too clearly for what it was: one of those badly sited, dull, ostentatious houses built at the end of the eighteenth century by people with more money than sense. For one thing the house was situated too near the brow of the hill—the down draught would be bound to make the fires smoke—and faced north. Wall the sloping kitchen garden as you might to keep off the bitter wind, there would be endless troubles with drainage and slugs.

Badger House—badgers prefer valleys, actually, but I daresay occasionally wander— was the property of Marigold's grandmother, Lady Hester Walpole Delingro. (Delingro had the money, she had the title; the marriage, her third, lasted six weeks.) But she kept the name, if only because it stood out in the gossip columns, and she loved a smart party, as did all the family. It was here at Badger House, every Christmas, that the whole vast, noisy, extroverted, once-Catholic Walpole family assembled to celebrate if not exactly the birth of Jesus (except perhaps for Marigold's 93-year-old great-aunt Cecilia, who was a nun, but whose convent let her out for Christmas), then their survival as a unit for another year.

The taxi let me out by the great front door. It was half past five on Christmas Eve. Heavy crimson damask curtains had been pulled, but there was an urgent sense of movement and life behind them. I rang three times and no one answered. I pushed the door open and went inside.

What noise, what brightness, what Babel! I would have turned and left at once and taken my chances on a train back to the city, but the taxi had already left. In the great hall someone was playing a grand piano honky-tonk style and a group of adults had gathered round to sing Christmas carols out of tune, rivalled only by a cluster of teenage children singing the pop world's seasonal offering, *Have Yourself a Hip-hop Xmas and Other Tunes,* and jigging about in ecstasy frenzy. Decorations were plentiful, but without discrimination, organization or style. Dull paper streamers, of the kind made by earnest children, hung droopily over great distances from wall to wall. Vulgar tinsel draped old family portraits, and cheap Woolworths magic lanterns in gold, silver, scarlet and green hung from chandeliers and doorways wherever the eye fell, without order and without symmetry. Little children were running around to no apparent purpose, the girls dragging Barbie dolls around by their hair and the boys panicking and shrieking, pursued by clanking and fashionably cursing computer toys they seemed unable or unwilling to control. Fires had been lit in all the rooms and, as I had predicted, smoked. I was obliged to pull my scarf up to cover my nose and mouth and breathe through that to save myself from the worst of the fumes.

As I stood there dazed and horrified, I was approached by Lady Hester. I recognized her from the pages of *Tatler* and *Hello*. (Yes, she stooped to *Hello*. I assumed that there were financial problems.) Lady Hester was a woman well into her eighties, still tall and gaunt, bright-eyed and vigorous for her age. She wore black leggings and a waisted silver jacket which would have looked better on a cheer-leader. Old legs are old legs and look skinny, not slender, and that's that.

'You must be Marigold's friend Ishtar,' she said. (My parents had been deeply into Middle Eastern mysticism around the time of my birth.) 'Welcome! I'm sorry about so much smoke. Very cunning of you to think of the scarf. As soon as the fireplaces warm up, it gets better. It's a problem we have every year. Part of the ritual!'

And just as Marigold came running up, I was saying 'Personally, I'd abandon the ritual and put in central heating,' which Lady Hester obviously did not react well to, if only because it was sensible advice. But Marigold hugged me and said, 'Ishtar, please don't tell the truth, remember it's Christmas. Let us have our illusions, if only for the weekend!'

I had never seen Marigold like this, as if she were 6 again, tippy-toed. Her usually pale horse face was flushed and she looked almost pretty. With tinsel in her hair, wearing a low-cut black top which left a bra-strap showing, she was knocking back the punch as if it were Diet Coke, hotly pursued by the Seb she sometimes talked about, a young man with curling golden tendrils clinging to a finely sculpted head.

'This is Ishtar,' she was saying to Seb, 'I share an office with her. She had nowhere to go for Christmas, so we've all agreed she can be this year's Outsider.'

Well, thank you very much, Marigold. Who wants to be labelled an Outsider, an object of pity, the one invited to the Christmas festivities because otherwise they'd be on their own? It seemed to me a gross abuse of the laws of hospitality and if thereafter I did not behave like a perfect guest, who can be surprised? Nor had I liked the way Seb's eye had drifted over me and away even before he had heard me described as the Outsider. Prada, to the uninformed eye, can sometimes look too plain, too dowdy.

But what did I do, you ask me, to justify some twenty people and a host of sticky little children bearing false witness against me? First remember that the Walpoles as a family are notoriously mentally unstable. They have become so through generations of mismarriages, drug-taking, miscegenation and eccentric social mobility. Rest assured that a girl who goes to the best school in the country is as likely to end up with a Rastafarian or a truck driver, as a stock broker or a prince. And that what kept them united was the worship of Lady Hester and the Christmas rituals over which she, as deity, presided.

I didn't do much; I just made sure that what I did was noticeable. Shown to an attic room with three makeshift beds in it, with twigs and soot tumbling down into the empty fireplace every time the door slammed (the chimneys were not even netted against the rooks), I explained that I would have insomnia if I did not have a bedroom to myself and that I needed sheets and blankets, not a duvet, and after much

175

apology and discussion ended up sleeping in Marigold's room and her on the sofa under the Christmas tree, so that Seb was unable to join her that night—I am sure that had been their plan—and the children did not get their normal sneak 2 a.m. preview of the presents.

People should not invite guests if they cannot house them adequately.

Earlier I'd found a gold dress in Marigold's wardrobe and put it on. Well, she offered.

'Isn't that one too tight? The navy would be more you.'

'Oh no,' I said. It was tight, of course, and incredibly vulgar too, but what does an Outsider know or care? I draped myself round Seb once or twice and pole-danced round a pillar for his entertainment. Then I let him kiss me long and hard under the mistletoe, while everyone watched. Marigold fled from the room weeping and flinging her engagement ring on the floor.

People who put up pagan mistletoe at a Christian ceremony must expect orgiastic behaviour.

Before going to bed I used the machines in the

utility room to launder the damp towels I had found on the floor of Marigold's bathroom. I had searched the linen cupboard for fresh ones but found none—what else could I do? The washing machine was faulty—there was no warning note to say so; is one meant to read the mind of machines?—and overflowed and caused some kind of havoc with the kitchen electrics, so the deep-freeze and the fridges cut out. This was not discovered until well into the next day.

People who stuff turkeys with packets of frozen pork and herbs deserve what they get and must risk E.coli if the power goes off.

On Christmas morning, leaving Seb in the bed, I rose early when only small hysterical children were about and restrained the ones who assaulted me too violently, or made me sticky, and escorted them to where their parents were sleeping in their drunken stupors and asked them to take charge of their offspring.

People should not have children if they do not have the moral wherewithal to control them.

I spent the morning assuring enquirers that Seb was nothing worth Marigold having, and in all probability was not her cousin but her half-brother, and preserving the Christmas presents from the ravages of the children, standing up to their wails and howls.

Then came the adult giving-ceremony. The custom was for every adult Walpole to bring what they called a tree-present, a gift acceptable to all ages and genders, to the value of £15, to place under the Christmas tree and when the time came to take another out for themselves. Thus everyone came with a gift and left with a gift. It was a system fraught with danger. Simply by taking one out and not putting one in, I caused mayhem. The nun Cecilia, being slowest on her feet, was left without a gift and made a terrible fuss.

Lunch did not happen until three. Some thirty people sat in a triangle formed by three trestle tables. The table setting, I must admit, was pretty enough and decorated with Christmas crackers and the heavy family silver had been taken out of storage. But thirty? How this family bred and bred!

I had been seated at the jutting end of one of the tables, as befitted the Outsider. This did not improve my mood. I declared myself to be a vegetarian just as the three turkeys—one for each side of the triangle—were being carved.

People who have thirty to a meal must surely expect a certain proportion of them to be vegetarians. I mentioned the deep-freeze débâcle, a number of the guests converted to vegetarianism there and then—all those, I noticed, who had married into the Walpole Delingros, those born into it were hardier.

Next to me was Cecilia, rendered incontinent by the morning's upsets. When all were finally served, I enquired what the strange smell could be. A faulty drain, perhaps? One or two got to their feet, and the children, seeing the adults rise, found the excuse to leave their chairs and run hither and thither, sniffing around under the table overexciting the dogs and pulling crackers out of turn.

People should look after the elderly properly and make sure they do not drink too much or lose control of their bladders.

It was at this point that Lady Hester Walpole Delingro rose to her feet and, pointing across the festive triangle at me, arm fully extended, asked me to leave her table, since it was clearly so unsatisfactory to me. I too rose to my feet.

'Thank you for making me your Outsider,' I said, 'at the annual feast of the Walpole Delingros. I would hate to be an Insider.'

This was no more than the truth, but Lady Hester's noble horse face contorted, reddened and went into spasms. She grabbed her heart, her hand fell away, she fell dead into her plate. It was over in five seconds. She can hardly have suffered. Rage and pain get confused. Nevertheless, it was a shock. Silence fell. Even the little children returned to their seats and sat silently.

And then something even more shocking occurred. A group of male Walpole Delingros carried off the body to the next room and stretched it out on the sofa under the Christmas tree, shut the door, returned to the table and behaved as if the death had not occurred. Lady Hester's plate was removed; her daughter, Lady Rowan, Marigold's mother, moved to fill the now empty chair. Everyone moved up one, even Cecilia, leaving me isolated but with one damp, smelly chair next to me.

'Shouldn't someone call a doctor, an ambulance?' I asked. No one replied. 'You can't just eat Christmas pudding as if nothing had happened!'

But they could. Curtains were drawn, lights put out, heated brandy poured over hot Xmas puddings to be set ablaze and carried in with ceremony. I was offered none. It was as if I had ceased to exist. Only after coffee had been made and served and crackers pulled—those the children had left—and the dreadful jokes been read out and scorned were the doctor, the ambulance and the police called.

And that, I swear, is exactly what happened. Even if thirty, not twenty, Walpole Delingros swear that the death happened after dinner and that I took Lady Hester's head and deliberately banged it on the edge of the marble fireplace during the course of an argument about the cause of smoking fireplaces, so she fell dead, suffering a cardiac infarction on the way down, I cannot help it. This was not what happened. If there is a nasty dent on the side of Lady Hester's head, why then, one of the family did it while she lay on the sofa, with a blunt instrument, the better to incriminate me.

It won't work, of course—one of the children must surely blab, or perhaps Marigold will remember she is my friend. I believe she is back with Seb. In the meantime, while I wait for my mother's call, I am happy enough in this cell.

But perhaps you could arrange to have *The Times* sent in, so that I can do the crossword? And could you ask the governor to stop people playing their radios and TVs so loudly? Or at any rate to tune them to the same station? I am feeling a little insecure. I am accustomed to having enemies—the honest and righteous always are—but it was my bad judgement to make so many, in one place, and in that particular season. It is never safe to disturb the ritual, however much fun it may be.

Moral

The honest and the righteous are a real pain to be with. They are the scribes and Pharisees you read about in the Bible. They are often friendless, and if you are a nice person you will feel inclined to ask them to share your family and social rituals, but remember virtue is its own reward.

Though actually there is a brighter side to virtue:

> Be happy and you'll be good, be
> good and you'll be happy.

Things turned out well for Marigold and really rather badly for Ishtar.

TWO

Saints and Sinners

Death, bereavement, loneliness and shame: these are the four horses of the modern apocalypse. They circle our new reality, now we are people of the city not the cave. Their riders, the horsemen, are a fearful lot: they are called despair, depression, isolation and self-doubt. But being so fearful they are easily unhorsed and it's simple enough to get out of their way. It's just not nice to find them champing the grasses in your back garden. You need to *do* something.

Skip these next few chapters if you are young, believe that none of these things will happen to you or in general believe that ignorance is best. You may be right. *Why know now what you can put off until tomorrow?*

The news is not totally good, though there are a few things here for your comfort. Your writer believes quite strongly in the afterlife and does not believe that when we die the light is switched off. It glimmers on elsewhere.

Our perceptions are based in our senses; our brains give us a mere three-dimensional readout. Mathematicians, whose models of the universe seem on the whole sound, give proof that other dimensions exist. This being the case, anything can happen, *and may well do.*

Angels and ministers of grace attend us!

Death: The Gates of Paradise

I have had various experiences of the 'other side'—enough to make me think that when people fear death, they really have no need.

I saw my one-time (a long-time) husband in the mortuary after he had died. He was cold like marble and had 'gone away'.

I sat by my mother while she died. Her attention turned inward; she forgot the world. She had no pain. She seemed to be learning something she was reluctant to learn, coming to terms with the end of life. The struggle was inward, with something I didn't understand, but it was resolved. But it was in no sense 'the end' when her eyes closed. She too had 'gone away'.

I had an out-of-body experience when I was in my mid-twenties, under anaesthetic. Lots of people have these and psychologists take pleasure in telling us 'Oh that's nothing but *an excitation of the pleasure centres of the brain!*' Though to me it seemed far too active an experience to be issuing from the brain cells, self-induced out of nothing.

187

I travelled down a warm dark tunnel—the birth canal, the romantics will tell you. If so, it was an easy journey, not punctuated by the squeezing of muscle and the compression of the head that must accompany birth from the baby's point of view. No wonder babies cry— they must all suffer from post-traumatic stress disorder for a long, long time, unless they are lifted gracefully and carefully from the womb by the surgeon. Doors opened on both sides as I travelled, and people came out to me, some I knew well, others I scarcely remembered, all in perfect form, spirit rather than body, and at their best, not their worst, so I was truly pleased to see them. I knew we were all in this together. At the end of the tunnel was a bright light, which was my destination—and then it faded and I woke up in my hospital bed. But it was enough to make me sure that 'the other side' existed, and I haven't worried about death since. But now I am not so sure. It might be more worrying than I, in my young naïvety, assumed.

Just a year ago I all but died from an allergic reaction. The hospital rang my family to say they'd better come quick. My heart had stopped. Crash teams worked on me and brought me back to life. I had a vision then of the gates of paradise. They filled edges of my vision and indeed they were pearly white but tinged with pink, merging into a rather vulgar orange and red—the colours you see in Hindu temples.

The gates were double-glazed and they slid aside a foot or two to give me room to enter and the inner space was filled with a kind of fog.

I was passing through, but then hands and voices struggled to hold me back, while from the other side some gaunt and terrifying creature with long limbs tried to entangle me and pull me through. I saw a drawing in a gallery recently by the German expressionist painter Kathe Kollwitz, done in the early 1930s. It was called 'Death and Child'. Death, long-armed, gaunt and determined, snatches the child from its mother's arms. And that, I realized, was a vision of what I had encountered. It is not all sweetness and light over there, at least it won't be for me. But there is, I am convinced, an over there. Kathe Kollwitz saw it too. You may do better than me. Angels may attend your entry. I hope so.

I asked my vicar whether he thought I had encountered Cerberus at the gates of hell. He said he hoped not.

The gates of paradise, I warn you, can be rather a shock to the aesthetic soul, trained to appreciate shades of taupe and stone and dim sepulchral gloom. Colour, on the other side, is vigorous and startling.

Nature is not your Friend

Lay the blame for the four enemies of happiness, the four new horses of the apocalypse—death, bereavement, loneliness and shame—at nature's door. All are attendant upon ageing. We can ameliorate their effects, but it is as well to acknowledge that nature is not our friend. Blithely, she discards us. Better treat her as an enemy. She is concerned with our children, not with us, and though our interests may overlap, they do not coincide. Nature has no interest in us once we are past a certain age—and even for the young she can prove an uneasy ally. She certainly takes no steps to make our endings happier, brittling our bones, drying our skin and rheuming our eyes.

It is misleading to personify her in the way I do, shorthand for the sum of cause and effect through the ages in the organic world. *'Nature wants us to do this, nature means us to do that'*—it leads us to believe that she knows what she is doing, that she is driving us forward to a perfect world. She is not. She just *is*. If she intends anything, it is for a tree to fall on us when we're 30, which we couldn't dodge in time because of our advancing years, or a pregnancy to kill off anyone remotely unfit, or starvation to carry off those not lucky enough to lay down fat in the good times.

'She' makes mistakes. Every mutation is a mistake. Occasionally these mistakes benefit humanity: we are far, far cleverer than we need be to survive. Nature, in her incompetence, has succeeded in breeding a race who need medicines to keep them going as they grew older, and as the centuries pass, and the fat beget the fat, a breed given to obesity. The advantage of being fat in the cave far outweighs any disadvantage.

In our later years nurture is thoroughly out of kilter with nature. We must stop thinking *'I won't take those pills, it isn't natural.' 'Nature wants us take exercise, so on my bike!' 'Surely it's the healthy option to have my baby in a field, as nature intended.'* What nature intended was that the weakest and oldest would die in childbirth. Not for nothing, in the days before pre-natal care became so sophisticated, was any woman over 30 called an 'elderly primigravida' and seen as being at special risk.

Our orthopaedic hospitals are full of elderly sportspersons who overtaxed their limbs in their youth and ageing ballet dancers with crumbling ankles. They had glorious youths— and good for them and it may well have been worth it. But old age goes on an awfully long time—medicine, interfering with nature's scheme for us, makes certain that it does.

(There is a theory that grandparents exist to help look after babies, that nature designed them so to do, but that seems to me to be pushing it. Nature is a blind, deaf, maddening, senseless, wholly amoral creature. 'Grandparent' is a term that applies to the world of nurture, not of nature, of central heating, fridges, telephones and steady heartbeats on CDs to soothe the baby. The heartbeats of the elderly aren't nearly as steady and reassuring as those of the young.)

Nature wins in the end and carries us off—though scientists are working on that too. There is a gene which plots the long-term destruction of all cells—'the suicide gene' they call it—and if they could only breed it out of humanity we could all be born, grow to our optimum size and just stay that way, never growing old. We could have our babies at the age of 106, 206, there being no inevitable ageing in our cells.

Then let them worry about elderly mothers.

If, of course, accident, global warming, floods and hurricanes, not to mention biological warfare, have spared us. Personally, I'd rather take the cloning option: it puts a bit more—not much more, but some—variety into the mix.

I wouldn't really be afraid of dying, if I were you. If wavering, open up Hubble on the Internet and consider the beauty and scale of the cosmos. Yet we can hold all this within our comprehension, and the smallest component of the atom too.

Nature, that imperfect energy, keeps the race going. It seems our souls need housing. The body withers and perishes, but the soul goes marching on, though God alone knows where. Somewhere in the starry void no doubt there's room. If infinity exists—and mathematicians keep telling us it does—everything is always *somewhere.*

Bereavement:
Unseating the Second Horseman

Forget the five stages of bereavement—traditionally denial, anger, bargaining, depression and acceptance—before the 'moving on', when you're meant to forget, start again as if nothing had happened. I think that's terrible. It's brainwashing. The dead are there to be remembered and honoured, not moved away from. They are still part of your life and times, even though their bodies are no more.

But time passes, other events crowd in. Treat grief like flu, something physical. Recovery is quicker—if 'recover' is what you want to do—if you understand the physicality of your own reaction. Don't seek forgetfulness—your loss is none the less because time passes—but normal life does need to resume. We have a duty to enjoy life, since we put such a premium upon it. Pleasure is the best weapon we have against the four horses and their riders. It is our answer to death. Rejoice! Bring out the best bottle of wine.

Grief is not a rational response to death; it is born out of instinct. It is to do with nature, not nurture. It is similar to bonding. If the baby is to survive, the mother needs to love and protect it. If a healthy young member of the tribe dies then he or she is out of the mating game. It won't do. Grief is nature's way (again the personification; I'm sorry, see it as shorthand) of making us careful that the tribe survives and the individual, and that this kind of thing doesn't happen too often.

Trapped submariners, stuck potholers, pile-ups on the motorway—see how the tribe rushes to help. Go into the trauma room in a hospital, see the shelves piled with boxes of this, packets of that, labels scrawled *'in case of this', 'in case of that'. 'Paediatric tracheotomy.' 'Adult appendectomy.'* It is the equivalent of having everything you might possibly need in an emergency in your pockets. Reason says, *'Let them die.'* Instinct says, *'Save at any cost!'* Terrific cost.

With the old we say, *'Well, they had a good life.'* We miss them, sometimes very badly, but we come to terms with it. When the young die, it is an outrage. Every quiver of our instinctive being rises up in protest. How will we live now? The cave echoes to our wails. Time fades grief as the power of bonding lessens—to an extent, never totally; nature is not so merciful—as the child grows.

See grief as to do with the survival of the tribe.

Mothers send sons off to war for the good of the tribe (well, they used to) more easily than they let them ride a motorbike. We grieve for our own, but rejoice at the death of the tribe over the hill. We even drop bombs on them. All the more for us! We can rush over the hill and steal the women, grab the genes and loot the caves.

To grieve for someone who dies isn't reasonable, it's just natural. Grief sweeps over us and absorbs us. It stops us functioning (unless other even more powerful instincts are at play, such as feeding the baby or killing the enemy). But those who have died have merely joined the ones who went before, as we all must do. They are beyond pain or grief of their own. We should be happy for them. It is reasonable for us to grieve for *ourselves*, because we've lost a parent, a lover, a child, a friend, and now have to do without them. But for them? Not really.

I once had a goose that died of grief for her gander. The fox got him. She wouldn't eat. She just walked about mournfully for a week and then sat down and breathed her last. Well, I understood that. I don't suppose she did. That's what I mean by instinct.

Depression: The Second Horseman

Death's rider is despair. Bereavement's is depression. What's worse, he has friends.

Free-floating Anxiety—Depression's Friend

Only to recognize this particular brand of anxiety for what it is can be helpful. It's not like ordinary anxiety, which is rooted in a particular circumstance. It's called 'free-floating' because it floats free like a cobweb of a bright morning, alighting here, alighting there. Free-floating anxiety is attracted like a magnet to real fears—betrayal, infidelity, growing old, suspicious pains, how to pay the bills—but if none of those are around it lands anywhere and you start worrying about whether you've got split ends and they're getting worse or why the children aren't back from a party. You know there is something that ought to be done, but you don't know what it is, and you can't quite locate the source of the anxiety because it's already floating off, attaching itself to something else in your head.

If it has the habit of alighting on you, you must treat it like flu—something disagreeable that goes away. Cosset yourself until it does. Go to bed early, have hot milky drinks, that kind of thing. (Unless the 'milky' makes you worry you're going to get fat, in which case make it hot water.)

Free-floating anxiety comes in different degrees: it can consume you, make your breath come in short gasps, be bad enough to give you pains in your stomach or trifling enough to make you restless because you're convinced your skin is feeling tight and you haven't got any moisturizer with you. Explain to yourself that this is a physical state. It's a sickness of the imagination. It will pass. Easier said than done, I know. But once I had the phrase 'free-floating anxiety' in my head, it ceased to be the plague it once was for me. Simply as if naming it was a talisman against impending disaster. Once I'd noticed how it alighted here, alighted there, it lost power. I could sit it out and wait for it to pass, and soon it lost interest and went away.

Know your enemy!

Another Friend
This is another good friend of depression—you're used to sex and it stops. A sudden cessation of sexual activity can bother a woman a lot, until she gets used to it. Here she is, in a nice home, long-time married, good relationship, children grown, roses growing in the garden or geraniums in the window boxes, sex calmer than once it was but still very much

ongoing. Then something *happens*—heart attack, stroke, prostate—and that's the dramatic end of that. Or else the sexual interest of the other just fades away.

And there you are, stranded. Life racing away at the speed of knots behind you.

The warmth and companionship of the double bed remains, and you don't want to disturb that, but unsatisfied longings swell in the loins, and you develop restlessness in the limbs, and it's amazing how much you can want something you can't have, at least within a normal domestic context.

When you had it you didn't take much notice of it. What can really bug you is what you haven't got.

So what do you do? Advice will vary on this point. Mine would be to put 'domestic' behind you. Develop a secret life while you still have the health and energy. Not too many questions will be asked if you go away for the odd weekend. Partners in these circumstances don't want to *know*, but they want you to be happy. Otherwise you might leave, and then what would they do?

Life is short; the grave is long. Just do it.

Use the Internet, use online dating agencies. Just do it.

If it all goes wrong, nothing is lost. You're old and experienced enough to tell a serial killer from a con man from a creep from a weirdo. And there are many, many people out there just like you, not wishing to disturb existing relationships, but longing to meet someone.

Loneliness:
Unseating the Third Horseman

Loneliness, the third horse of the apocalypse, is the one most of us fear the most, and rightly.

Loneliness can strike at any time. Even when you're in your prime. It's terrible. We are people of the tribe, happiest when clustering with others. Sometimes we can't. Sometimes we don't want to—we would rather be right than sociable, as was the girl who wrecked the Christmas party in the parable. Sometimes we have brought it on ourselves; sometimes we can't help it.

The Loneliness of Youth

It can happen when we are young. In our teenage years. You change schools, you know no one. The friends you have gang up on you. Boyfriends reject you, teachers hate you, your mother quarrels with you, your father's left home. There's nobody to talk to. Just when you need to talk about yourself the most, just when you're at your solipsistic zenith, there's no one to talk to. That's bad.

(I was bought up in a world where there were no teenagers. The word did not yet exist. We belonged to the coy and discreet world of the young unmarried girl, who the tribe dictated should be shy and self-effacing. Then nurture came along and moulded us into a market and gave us consumer power and self-determination. But nature still gets through to us, and when it does we suffer.)

But at least when you're young loneliness passes. There is time for things to change, for friends to court you, boyfriends to want you, teachers to admire you, your mother to forgive you, your father to return—and then all you'll want is a bit of peace and quiet. *'I want to be alone,'* you'll cry.

The Loneliness of Later On

You move house. Friends drift away. You work from home. (You never much enjoyed the company of other women and it seemed such an opportunity. Now you wonder.) Children leave home. Husbands go, or you throw them out, for good reasons or bad. Then you rather wish you hadn't. You quarrel with your mother and think she should be the one to apologize first.

You have everything you need. You have done very well in the world. You are warm, housed, clothed, fed and safe. How those in the cave would envy you if they could see you now. This is the world that the men of the tribe built, for good or bad, by their incessant tinkering, their curiosity and their craving for power, a world far above and beyond the needs of survival, just as the peacock's tail is double the size needed to attract a mate.

(This is not to say that women freed from ill health and child bearing and rearing would not have invented television and the space shuttle. But I doubt it. Really, from a woman's point of view, these things are rather absurd and unnecessary. Television, mind you, is a good babysitter, as is a computer. It might have happened.)

Thanks to your own efforts, building upon those of others in ages past, your house is smart, your TV screen large, your iPod perfect. You wear Prada, there's a delicatessen next door, you have money in the bank, you have intimidated your suitors so they don't call and you have a pension. You have everything you want, but you don't want it any more. Because if you don't have friends it adds up to a string of beans.

Without people to talk to, without family, friends and colleagues, you can begin to believe you don't exist. We define ourselves as the sea defines the shore and the shore defines the sea: by the people around us. Speak to no one all day and then say hello to the girl in the supermarket, and your voice belongs to a stranger.

Solutions

Of course there are solutions to loneliness, namely (mostly) other people. You can go to a gym and while honing your perfect body to more perfection still you can pick up a friend or two there.

Or you can let yourself grow fat. People are nicer to you if they feel sorry for you and don't have to envy you. You could make a friend of the girl in the supermarket while discussing different brands of chocolate.

Try the Internet. In the chat rooms you can be who you like, change your gender, invent a history, be a fictional person, hook up with others as fictional as you are. As long as you don't assume anyone is speaking the truth about anything, there is no harm in it. A friend of mine, an actress, now aged 63, after a lifetime of emotional disasters met a museum curator on the Internet and developed a suitable interest in archaeology and now they live in married tranquillity at the foot of a Stone Age fort in the West Country. He really was a museum curator, GSOH, NS, just rather shy. She'd lied about her age, said she loved animals when she didn't, said she'd been married three times when it was five, and so on. When she met him she told the truth and he didn't seem to mind at all.

Inviting the Third Horseman In

Some people do it. It's madness. They quarrel with others. What's that but inviting loneliness in? They may not see it as quarrelling, just as a reasonable response to other people's bad behaviour, but they end up lonely just the same. The horse of loneliness champs and paws outside their front door. He's a grey and steely nag, rather thin and dour. Isolation, the third horseman, dismounts and knocks. And there's no one to answer. It's like the Walter de la Mare poem *The Listeners*, where the Traveller's horse champs the grasses of the forest's ferny floor, and he knocks upon the door a second time but still no one answers.

(My grandmother, who knew Walter de la Mare, said to me once, when I quoted the poem to her, *'Yes, and if they knew it was Walter standing out there I'm not surprised they didn't answer.'* I don't know what she had against the poet. Perhaps he just wasn't very affable.)

What you don't want is the lonely horse and the lonely rider to come sniffing around your door. Both have gaunt, wild and terrible eyes and bony ribs. They don't like friends. They don't like family, particularly mothers. If they get a whiff of real maternal concern, they're off. Never, never quarrel with your mother. It is no use being censorious about them; mothers are the source of your life.

Being Lonely in Company

Being lonely in company is almost worse than being lonely on your own. You have done everything you can to keep the third horse away, but still he stays, champing the grass on the forest's ferny floor. And the chatter of small children and the booming of a male voice can add up to an oppressive stillness in the air.

It is possible to be lonely when there are quite a lot of people in the house—when no one understands anything you say, when the children are too small to conduct a conversation, though they chatter and fill your head with noise, when your husband doesn't seem to know you're there, and even seems to wish you weren't.

It happens.

And then I think it is understandable if you leave. The female heart can only stand so much unhappiness.

This is another true story of what once happened at Schiphol. I love Schiphol, Amsterdam's airport. It seems to be a place where the convergent dynamics of many lives meet and make sense. In the swirl of humanity you begin to see patterns. It is the nexus of the new world.

Why Did She Do That?

Sooner or later all roads lead to Schiphol Airport, if only for an hour or so, on the way from here to there, in transit.

We perched on high stools at the Oyster Bar where zones C and D meet. My husband had a new-season herring and a glass of beer and I had a brown shrimp sandwich and a modest glass of white wine. After that we planned to go to the art exhibition in the new extension of Rijksmuseum situated where Zone E meets Zone F. The exhibits change every month or so and there is always some new skating scene, some famous soldier on a horse, some soothing Dutch interior to be seen, some long-dead artist's glimpse of that love and trust that exists within families or between mankind and nature. Thus fortified, we would fly on to Oslo, or Copenhagen, or on occasion further afield along those curving, separating lines on the KLM map— Bombay, Los Angeles, Rio de Janeiro, Perth, wherever.

And if we were lucky, on the return journey the Rijksmuseum exhibits would have been changed and there would be yet more to see. That is, of course, if delays and security checks allowed us the time we expected to have to spare in that strange no-man's land called Transit.

Lucky, I say, but thinking about it I am not sure. The paintings in the Rijksmuseum pull you out of the trance that sensible people enter while travelling, checking out from real life the moment they step into the airport and coming back to full consciousness only when once more entering their front door. The technical name for the state is derealization, or dissociative disorder. Too much of it, they say, and you can actually shrink your hippocampus, that part of the brain from which the emotions fan like airline flight paths on the map, never to recover. It might be wiser just to stare at the departure board like anyone else.

But I am with my husband, a rare bird who has never in his life experienced a dissociative state, and is enjoying his herring, and I am emerging from mine in preparation for the Rijksmuseum and am even vaguely wondering whether I am drinking Chardonnay or Chablis when there is a sudden commotion amongst the throng of passengers.

The Oyster Bar is by a jeweller's booth, where today there are diamonds on special offer. *'The new multi-faceted computer cut'*—whatever that might be. Presumably habitual buyers of diamonds know. But can there be so many of them as the existence of this shop suggests—so many enthusiastic or remorseful husbands or lovers who want to buy peace and stop off to purchase these tokens of respect and adoration? Though I daresay these days travelling women buy diamonds for themselves.

Next to the diamond boutique is a shop selling luggage and a booth offering amaryllis bulbs at ten euros for two. As a point-of-sale feature I see they're using a reproduction of that wonderful early Mondrian painting you can see in the Museum of Modern Art in New York, 'Red Amaryllis with blue background.' I bet that cost them a bit. It's midday by now and comparatively quiet in Schiphol, few customers and lots of staff, like a church when the congregation has left after a big service and the clerics are busy snuffing out candles and changing altar cloths. How do these places ever make a living? It defeats me.

A woman and her husband walk past us in the direction of departure gates C5–C57. They are in their forties, I suppose. I notice her because she walks just a little behind him and I tend to do the same whenever I am with a man. It is a habit which annoys husbands, suggesting as it does too much dependency, too little togetherness, but in a crowded place it seems to me practical. You don't have to cut a swathe through potentially hostile crowds, and passage can be effected in single file.

Couples who face the world side by side, I am prepared to argue, assert coupledom at the expense of efficiency. And it must be remembered that Jacob sent his womenfolk to walk before him when angry neighbours obliged him to return to Esau and the family farm, so that the wrath of Esau would fall first upon the wives and not upon him. As it happened Esau wasn't in the least angry about the business of the potage and was simply glad to see his long-lost brother again. But lagging behind is always safest in a world scattered with landmines both real and metaphorical. This woman seemed well aware of their existence.

I was hard put to decide their nationality. Probably British, certainly northern European. They had a troubled air, as if worried by too much debt and too little time ever to do quite what they wanted to do, always grasping for something out of reach, disappointed by the world, not as young as they'd like to be or as rich as they deserved to be. I blame the Calvinists and the work ethic: people from the warmer south have easier ways, less conscience and more generous hearts. Something at any rate was wrong. The flight had been delayed, or it was the wrong flight, or they didn't really want to go where they were going, or they didn't want to go together, or she was thinking of her lover or he of his mistress. But I didn't expect what was to happen next.

She was, I suppose, in her mid-forties: a respectable, rather pudding-faced, high-complexioned, slightly overweight stolid blonde with good legs and expensive hair piled up untidily in a bun. She was trying too hard. Her skirt was too tight and her heels too high and slim for comfortable travel. She wore a pastel pink suit with large gold buttons. The jacket stretched a little over a middle-aged bosom, that is, it was no longer perky but bulged rather at the edges. She carried a large shiny black plastic bag.

The husband who walked before her looked like a not-very-successful businessman: he wore jeans, a tie and a leather jacket, not high street but not Armani either, and you felt he would be happier in a suit. His face was set in an expression of dissatisfaction, his hair was thinning, he had the air of one beset by responsibilities and the follies of others. There was no doubt in my mind that they were married. How does one always know this? We will leave that as a rhetorical question, it being parried only with another: 'Why else would they be together?'—and the import of that exchange is too sad to contemplate.

But I thought of that tender 1641 Van Dyke painting of the newly married pair, William, Prince of Orange, aged 15, and Mary, Princess Royal of England, aged 10, and took comfort. The weight of the world is upon the young pair, and all the troubles of state and domesticity, and they are brave and beautiful in the face of it. And I sipped my Chardonnay, or Chablis, and watched the couple walk by, and wondered about their lives. They were on their way, perhaps, to visit a first grandchild and had never approved of the marriage in the first place, or to visit her parents, whom he had never liked. Something like that.

And then one moment she is walking beside him—well, a little behind him, as I say—and he says something and she suddenly falls on her knees before him. It is quite a movement: she seems to shoot out from behind him to arrive at floor level, twisting to face him. It is the same movement you see in the Pinter play, *Homecoming* I think it is, the one in which the man proposes to the woman, shooting right across the stage on his knees to entreat her to be his.

A few years back, when Harold Pinter was playing the part himself at the Almeida theatre, he remarked at one of those theatre evenings when the audience quizzes those on stage that his knees were no longer up to it. He was 60. The part really needed a younger man. I stood up in the audience and proposed a solution, namely that he altered the part to suit his knees. Let the actor propose from a sitting position and write a few lines to convey the power of the entreaty. It was, after all, his play. He could do what he liked with it. But the playwright was shocked and I sat down reproached. The lines were sacrosanct, they had entered into the canon, they were no longer Pinter's to change. They were derealized, they dwelt with other sacred texts in some dissociated state of their own, stage directions which had to be served and suffered for, by the writer too. I really admired that.

Picture the scene that day at Schiphol. Now the woman is wailing aloud like an animal, a human bereft, a cow that has lost its calf, hands clasped towards her husband in entreaty, her hair toppled around her face, her red-lipsticked mouth smeary and gaping wide, her back teeth dark with old-fashioned fillings. Her heels stick out oddly at the end of lean shins, as if someone had broken her bones, but people's legs do look like that sometimes when they kneel at the communion rail. Her skirt is rucked up, too tight and short for this sudden, passionate, noisy activity. She is not like a virgin, beautiful in prayer; she is a fat middle-aged woman with thin legs having a mad fit. She is praying to him, beseeching him, *'Have mercy. Lord, have mercy. Angels and ministers of grace attend me!'*

At the Oyster Bar glasses pause mid-air. People all around pause in their transit and look to see what's going on. The husband takes a pace or two back, embarrassed and bewildered, and stares at the wife. He is trying to look as if she is nothing to do with him. At least he does not disappear into the crowd. Perhaps she has his passport.

Something stranger still happens. Women staff come out of the shops, first hesitantly, then with more deliberation, and move towards the source of the noise. There are two young girls with bare midriffs, but most are brisk and elegant older women in crisp white shirts and black skirts and sensible shoes. They cluster round the wife, they help her to her feet, they brush her down, soothing, clucking, sympathizing. She stops the wailing, looks round their kindly, consoling faces. She feels better. She manages a tremulous smile.

An armed policeman approaches. He is dismissed by this Greek chorus of female nurturers with a look, a dismissive flick of a hand, a derisive finger, and he melts away. It occurs to me that the Nurturers, even more difficult to sight than the Norns, who weave the entrails of Nordic heroes to decide their destiny, or those Mediterranean Furies, who drive us mad with guilt, have actually put in an appearance at Schiphol. Like the Lover at the Gate, unseen until the hour of need, who fills up the bed when the husband departs, these benign creatures turn up in an emergency, so long as it is dire enough. I have always suspected they existed, though unsung in fable, but I had never sighted them until now. And in an airport! I am privileged.

Then, as if this was her destined fate and this was their purpose, the Nurturers propel the woman towards her waiting husband. She does not resist. She is tentative and apologetic in demeanour. The expression on his face does not change: *'I am a man beset by troubles, bravely enduring.'*

The Nurturers turn back into shop assistants and disappear behind their counters. The couple walk on as if nothing had happened, towards Zone C, she is still just a little behind him. She pushes her hair back into its proper shape and wobbles on her heels. She may have hurt her knees.

Back at the Oyster Bar things return to normal. Eating and drinking continue. The crowds close behind the couple. Schiphol flows on. Lunchtime is approaching, noise levels are increasing.

'Why did she do that?' my husband asks, bewildered. 'Is she mad?'

'He may well have driven her mad,' I say. 'She will not have got there on her own.'

216

And as we make our way to the Rijksmuseum, I tell him how I imagine the day has gone for the blonde woman and how she has been driven to distraction, to the point of falling upon her knees in a public place and wailing, imploring her husband to stop, just stop, her state of desperation so extreme that she managed to summon the Nurturers. What I tell him is, of course, only one of a dozen possible scenarios.

'Marcelle,' he said to her this morning—I will call her Marcelle, she looked like a Marcelle, and we will call him Joseph, perhaps in the spirit of mild irony. Joseph, after all, stood steadily stood by Mary in the hour of her need: he did not take a step back and try to disown her when she embarrassed him so— 'Marcelle, did you remember to call Sylvia about Alec last night?'

Marcelle is busy packing a suitcase not quite big enough for all her needs. They are up early. They have a flight to catch.

Marcelle and Joseph will live in a detached house with thick carpets and good reproduction furniture and a designer kitchen. He will have one married daughter by an earlier marriage and they will have two teenage children between them and a neat garden in which anything unruly will have been cut down to size. She will use bark chippings, that ugly stuff, to keep the weeds down.

Joseph: 'Ugly, what do you mean, ugly? Well, you should know. But I am not made of money. We cannot afford a gardener more than once a week, for God's sake.'

Once, long ago, Marcelle dreamed of romance and roses round a cottage door, and once indeed Joseph picked a single cherry in an orchard and brought it to her. That was when she was first pregnant with Alec and Joseph was emotional about it. She kept the pip for ages and even tried to make it sprout by putting it in water. Then she would have a whole little tree covered with cherries, but nothing happened except that the pip just lay there and the water grew cloudy and sour and she had to throw it out. All that was left was a ring round the glass which no amount of scouring would remove. Still, even that was something. A memento of something good.

She would really like another suitcase just for her cosmetics, but Joseph doesn't like heaving cases about. Who does? Jars are heavy and bulky, and creams for the eyes and the neck and the lips and the bust are probably interchangeable, but she is nervous of being without a single one of them. She can't make up her mind. She packs and repacks. She slips jars into her shoes to save space, but the weight is unavoidable.

Joseph: 'Couldn't you do without the gunk for just a couple of days and nights? It's not as if it seems to make any difference. You're over 40, nearly 50. Surely the days when face creams would help have passed? Take them to the charity shop and be rid of them.'

As if charity shops took half-empty jars of cream, however expensive. What do men know?

'I called but there was no answer,' lies Marcelle.

'Did you leave a message on Sylvia's answerphone?' asks Joseph. He has already packed. It takes him five minutes. He is decisive.

Joseph: 'One of us has to be.'

Now he is brushing his teeth. Marcelle cooked him breakfast but had none herself. He likes a good breakfast; she is never hungry first thing in the morning. Joseph has good teeth; Marcelle spends a lot of time at the dentist.

Joseph: 'My mother made sure I had milk every day. You really shouldn't let Alec and Carla drink those disgusting sweet drinks all the time. It's not as if they have particularly good dental genes—at least not from your side.'

But how do you stop teenagers from eating and drinking exactly what they want? It wasn't as if Joseph was around all that much at mealtimes to train them to do anything at all, let alone sit down when they ate and drank.

'I couldn't,' says Marcelle. 'It wasn't switched on.'

'That's strange,' says Joseph. 'Sylvia is usually so efficient.'

According to Joseph, Sylvia is elegant, Sylvia is intelligent, Sylvia has perfect teeth. What a good dress sense Sylvia has. So slim! Such a pretty figure. Sylvia is like a sister to Joseph, and tells everyone so, though of course they are no blood relation. Sylvia has twin girls of 15 who are very smart and well behaved and no trouble at all.

Joseph: 'Sylvia knows how to bring up children.'

The only thing wrong with Sylvia is her husband Earle. Joseph thinks Earle is something of a slob, not worthy of Sylvia. Earle and Sylvia are Joseph and Marcelle's best friends, and their children like to spend time together. But over the last five years Earle has crept up the promotion ladder and Joseph has stuck on a certain rung while others have clambered up over him.

The fact is, Marcelle did not want to call Sylvia. It was late, she was tired, and now, thank God, it is too early.

Seven years ago Joseph spent a night with Sylvia in a hotel at a sales conference. He had come home in the morning smelling of Sylvia's scent.

Joseph: 'Why do you never wear scent any more, Marcelle?'

Marcelle: 'Because I am too busy. Because I never remember to wear it. Because it made the babies sneeze and I got out of the habit.'

Then he had confessed and apologized and Marcelle and Sylvia had talked it out and had agreed to forget the incident, which had been, well, yes, both unfortunate and unexpected.

> *Joseph: 'I am so sorry, Marcelle. It should not have happened. But she is such a honey, such a sweet dear, you know how much you like her, and she is having such a hard time with Earle. I can only conclude somebody put something in the drink or it would never have happened. It meant nothing—it was just a silly physical thing. And she is your friend. I feel much better now I've told you.'*

Yes, but in a hotel? A whole night? Full sex? Behind the filing cabinets would have been more understandable.

> *Sylvia: 'I am so, so sorry, Marcelle. I would never do anything to hurt you. I will always be open with you. It was a silly drunken thing—someone must have put something in the office drink. It was completely out of character and will never happen again. We both have our marriages and our children to think about, so shall we both just say "closure" and forgive and forget?'*

So Marcelle had. Or had tried to.

Sylvia was a psychotherapist who worked in the human resources department of the haulage business where Joseph worked as an accountant. Earl was now director of acquisitions at the same firm, earned far more than Joseph and had an office to himself and a good carpet. He was away from home quite a lot visiting subsidiary companies abroad. Sylvia was brave about his absences but sometimes she would turn up at Marcelle's door at the weekend with red eyes and talk about nothing in particular and Marcelle felt for her. And Marcelle could see that bedding Sylvia had been a triumph for Joseph, a feather in his cap, so great an event it was now what sustained him in life.

Joseph: I was the one who bedded Sylvia, Earle's wife, at the office party seven years ago.

But Marcelle still did not want to call Sylvia about Alec. Alec had been found taking drugs at school and was in danger of expulsion. Joseph reckoned that Sylvia could help with advice and wisdom. She after all being so good with young people. Her twins would never take drugs, or be anorexic, like Carla. They were calm and orderly and dull.

'I'll call her when we get back from Copenhagen,' Marcelle says to Joseph, looking up from the parade of jars: different makes, different shapes, some gold-topped, some white, some silvery, all enticing. They are going to visit the new baby and will only be staying two days. She is glad it is not longer. Her step-daughter has always been a bundle of resentments at the best of times. Now she will be sleepless and ordering Marcelle about as if she were the maid.

Joseph: 'What can you expect? You stole me from her. Now you have to put up with it.'

It will not be an easy trip. Joseph does not like the new husband.

'That's all very well,' Joseph says to Marcelle, 'but you promised me you'd call her and now you haven't. I really don't understand you.'

'I expect it will have blown over by the time we get back,' says Marcelle with unusual firmness. 'Schools always over-react. And I really I don't see why Sylvia needs to know every detail of our business.'

'She's a good friend to you,' says Joseph. 'Better than you'll ever know.'

What does he mean by that? Has something else happened between Joseph and Sylvia? Has he tried to restart the flirtation and she refused, for Marcelle's sake? Or is that just what Joseph wants Marcelle to think, because he's annoyed?

She gives up on the throat cream and then thinks of Sylvia's smooth and perfect neck and repacks it. Perhaps she can do without the eye cream? Sylvia is seven years younger than Marcelle. Sylvia has beautiful clear bright eyes, widely spaced, and good cheekbones. Flesh seems somehow to have shrouded Marcelle's.

She feels suddenly hungry and goes to the kitchen to have a cup of coffee and a piece of toast. Joseph follows her into the kitchen.

'Sylvia says the way to keep slim is never to eat carbohydrates before breakfast,' he observes. 'And I don't think this matter of Alec is simply going to melt away, however much you hope it will. You have such a problem with reality! I don't like to say this of Alec, but there is a history of criminality in the family. Remember the time when he was eight and you found money missing from your purse? I don't think you dealt with that properly. Sylvia said the whole thing should have been talked through, not just swept under the carpet. Now this drugs business. Where has the boy been getting the money?'

Marcelle's father, a respectable builder, had served four months in prison for petty theft very shortly after Joseph and Marcelle were married. He had taken a lathe home, he said by accident, but the client had reported it to the police and the magistrate, no doubt in the middle of his own building work, had seen it as a gross breach of trust.

Marcelle had always had an uneasy suspicion that if her father had turned into a jailbird before the wedding, not after, it would never have taken place. Somehow the feeling was always there that she was lucky to have caught Joseph—a surgeon's son, well educated, good-looking, an accountant with a degree in mathematics. Joseph's family photographs were in real silver frames. Marcelle's were in plastic.

She saw herself with a terrible clarity: good legs and bosom, but with a tendency to put on weight, no conversation, no dress sense, no brains and no qualifications, a too-shrill speaking voice and a vulgar laugh. And both children took after her, not him. They were a disappointment to Joseph. If he'd married someone like Sylvia, one of whose sisters was now the wife of a peer of the realm, albeit non-hereditary, he would have had children as perfect as the twins. Though Earle had once said something really nice when they were round to dinner.

Earle: 'Say what you like about those children of yours, Marcelle, they're never dull. They're like you—a pleasure to be with.'

Marcelle had been serving a chocolate mousse at the time. Sylvia never served sweets, only cheese. She didn't believe in sugar. Sylvia had made quite a face when Earle had said that to Marcelle and had looked disdainfully at the mousse and tried to smirk at Joseph, but Joseph for once had taken no notice. He had even seemed pleased at what Earle had said, as if he too were being complimented. Men were strange. They were pack animals, no doubt about it, and very aware of who was top dog. Sometimes Marcelle was surprised that Joseph had never actually offered her to Earle in recompense for the office party incident, just to even things out. She wouldn't have minded too much if he had; she liked Earle. But Sylvia would not have liked it one bit.

Marcelle knows Joseph loves her, and she certainly loves him. She feels for him acutely as the world looks by him and over him. She wants to protect him. She knows why he is trying to upset and disturb her: there was a letter in the post recently about his pension and the assumption was that he had reached the ceiling of his career and would never earn more than he did now. They will never have a swimming pool like Earle and Sylvia. They will have each other, of course, but that in itself is a disappointment to Joseph. How can it not be? There are so many beautiful and brilliant women in the world that will never be his.

Marcelle also worries about Alec and Carla, because Joseph cuts them down to size all the time, as he does her, and she knows that children grow into their parents' plan for them. She wishes that he would just sometimes *pretend* to love and admire them more. It would help them.

'I hope you're going to change before we leave?' he asks. She is wearing black trousers and a dark-blue cashmere sweater, soft and comfortable but rather over-washed.

'I wasn't going to,' she says.

'Why don't you wear that nice pink thing? Sylvia always says how much it suits you.'

She changes into the pink suit, which is too tight for her and makes her look vast. She has not worn it for a few months. She can't admit it's unwearable, she will only get a lecture on Sylvia and carbohydrates. She will just have to hope Joseph doesn't notice.

She goes back into the kitchen. He looks her up and down and says nothing. He is not looking forward to the trip, either. His son-in-law is a man he does not like or respect. He is a small-time Danish architect who came to Marcelle and Joseph's house to discuss plans for a conservatory in the days when they could have afforded one. The plans came to nothing, but he went away with the daughter.

Joseph: 'Marcelle, I can't forgive you for this! When you knew they were seeing each other, why didn't you stop them? It's a disaster.'

Now he has to go and see the baby, fruit of this union, and try and look pleased. He never saw himself as a grandfather.

'Well, I don't want to be a grandmother either,' thinks Marcelle, with a sudden burst of inner petulance. 'Two can play at this game, and it's your fault, not mine, that I am, since I married a man with a child, more fool me.' She knows better than to say so. She takes a spoonful of conserve straight from the pot and puts it into her mouth without even bothering about the toast, and Joseph, with a sharp intake of breath, leaves the room.

Marcelle solves the beauty problem by slipping such small jars as she can into the case of Joseph's laptop. With any luck he won't notice the extra weight. She wears her highest heels. She knows they are impractical for travel, but her morale needs boosting. Since the only good thing about her that Joseph is prepared to admit to at the moment is her legs, she will make the most of them. Sylvia may have the eyes and the cheekbones and the salary, but Marcelle has the legs.

They get to the airport in good time. Joseph cannot abide being in a rush and Marcelle has learned not to hold him up. She has to pay extra because her bag is so heavy.

Joseph (the week after the wedding): 'Now, about our finances. We will each pay proportionate to our earnings and keep careful and accurate accounts. I will be paying the lion's share out of the joint account, but that is right and proper: I am your husband. I am not complaining. Personal extras must come out of our separate accounts—by "extras" I mean jaunts to the café, having your friends to lunch, parking fines, excess luggage, petrol for unnecessary outings, that sort of thing.'

And Marcelle had agreed, without asking for clarification as to who decided on the interpretation of 'unnecessary'. Her mother had told her at the time to get everything straight within the first week of marriage because if it wasn't done then it never would be. But that had been the week her father had gone to prison and her mother had been told she had cancer. She hadn't been concentrating.

On the Cityhopper flight to Schiphol Joseph said, 'I am disappointed you didn't get through to Sylvia. It's very unusual for her to leave the answerphone switched off. When we get to Amsterdam I'll call her on her mobile and you can talk to her then.'

'Did you bring the number with you?'

'It's on my mobile,' he pointed out.

'Well, it would be, wouldn't it?' Marcelle said. That was rash.

'I don't know what's the matter with you,' he said, looking at her with disdain. 'Next thing you'll be wanting to go through my numbers called to check up on me and Sylvia. It really is sick, Marcelle. So jealous of your best friend you'd risk the future of your own son! And your mascara has gone odd. There are

231

little lumps of it under your left eye. Why do women want to plaster their faces with that stuff? It makes them look worse, not better.'

She could have pointed out that Alec was his son too, and if he were so sure Sylvia would know how to deal with the situation he could always have called her himself, or popped into her office for a consultation on how to conduct his family affairs. No doubt he did that all the time, anyway. But she said nothing. There was a strange kind of bubbling feeling inside her. Was this what blood boiling felt like? Her ears popped as the aircraft began to descend and she felt more normal again.

Joseph called Sylvia from Schiphol to check up on the status of her phone and Sylvia reported that it was fine, as far as she knew. Perhaps Marcelle had dialled a wrong number. It was easy to do, they made the keys so small these days. She'd be delighted to talk to Marcelle about Alec—when they got to Copenhagen, perhaps, and had a little more time. It might be that Marcelle was the troubled one, not Alec?

'Did you hear that, Marcelle?' asked Joseph. 'You might be the troubled one, not Alec. We'll have to think about that. Sylvia always has a fresh slant on things. I knew we ought to talk to her.'

Joseph and Marcelle made their way towards the gate for the Copenhagen flight. After the brief good cheer of his conversation with Sylvia, Joseph's mood was worsening.

'I wish you'd keep up, Marcelle. And why are you wearing those stupid shoes? And pastel pink? For travelling? The skirt's too short for someone your age and weight. You look absurd. The only gold buttons in this whole airport belong to you. Sometimes I think you do it on purpose.'

And that was the point at which she threw herself on the ground in front of him, on her knees, hands clasped like a supplicant, wailing, *'Stop it, stop it, stop it, come back to me, love of my life!'* so piercingly loud in her heart that the Nurturers heard and came to her rescue and returned her to him and him to her.

These things can happen beneath our very noses. I like to think that so shocked was he, so brought to his senses, that he didn't say a single mean thing to Marcelle, or even mention Sylvia, for the rest of the visit. That he even picked up the baby—it was a girl— and smiled at it and said, 'You're a pretty girl, just like your grandmother. And you have her lovely smile.'

'So that's why she did it,' I said to my husband. 'He drove her mad.'

'It's obvious you can't resist a happy ending,' he said. 'Personally, I felt very sorry for the poor man. I hope she's ashamed of herself.'

By that time we were at the Rijksmuseum, but found it was closed, because they were changing the paintings.

Shame:
Unseating the Fourth Horseman

The fourth horse of the new apocalypse is shame and his rider is self-doubt. A nasty, shabby pair.

These days the nag shame tends to get called 'low self-esteem'. It's when you have nothing to be proud of and you know it, when you leave the house with your head lowered because of the spots, wearing dark glasses because you think your eyes are too small and go to bed with anyone who asks you because (others say) your Darwinian sense of selection, your ambition to win an alpha male, has somehow been eroded. When other women say, *'Poor thing, such low self-esteem, she's anyone's.'* When you overhear some young man, rightly nervous about his sexual prowess, talk about *'a charity fuck'* and you realize he means you.

That wouldn't be too good for your self-esteem. Your argument—that you just like sex, that's why you do it—might sound a little weak, for a time. But it's just as likely to be true. You do it because you like it, nothing to do with low self-esteem.

Shout it to the rooftops and shame will gallop off into the night, with his rider self-doubt mumbling into his high collar as he goes, skeletal bones glimmering in the night, *'What I need is a people-carrier. I'm ashamed to be seen on this old nag.'*

But don't tell your fiancé too much about all this. You are a new improved person now.

More Irresponsible Advice

We are not pursuing happiness here, but survival. These actions require secrecy; you must never tell anyone. They are least-worst options, not good in themselves, but the best solution in the circumstances. For example I would say it was allowable to cheat on your husband/boyfriend when higher things were at stake. That is to say the preservation of your home/relationship/sanity.

I must warn you, in passing, that in my experience most significant secrets of a sexual nature are in the end revealed, but with any luck decades will pass before they are and perhaps then it won't matter so much.

But beware the deathbed confession:

He: 'Rita, I slept with Margie 30 years ago.'

When Rita's his wife and you're Margie. And
the scandal gets round the retirement home.
Well, at least you had a past.

Beware the brink-of-divorce disclosure:

She: 'And what is more I slept with Tom,
Dick, Harry and Edward, and every single
one of them was better in bed than you.'

It may be true, but twenty-four words can
cost you a fortune in alimony.

Beware the impetuous desire to confess:

He: 'I have to tell you, Robert, it keeps me
awake at night: I slept with your wife seven
years back.'

Especially if you are Robert's wife. Some
people can never just leave well alone.

Nevertheless, there are risks you may
sometimes have to take.

On Not Having a Baby When You Want One

It hasn't happened naturally and all your
friends seem to have one. You're in a bad
situation: the solution is going to be least-
worst. And it will not get better on its own.

You have waited five years already.

(Sometimes waiting another ten works. So convinced was one of my friends after fifteen years that she was infertile, she took no precautions and suddenly, at 44, she was pregnant. Three cats had to go, and two dogs and a parrot. Psittacosis! And their pension scheme, and her job, and their three holidays a year . . . However. They went through with it. It is the most darling baby. But that's by the by.)

You may well blame yourself. *'I should have started earlier.'* Well, you didn't. Too bad. But that's in the past. And anyway, it might have nothing to do with you, it could be him. It might be his fertility that's in question.

You can start down the long gruelling road of treatment, surrender yourself and your partner to internal investigation, the humiliation of body and soul for an uncertain end—quite possibly ending up with neither partner nor child—or you can try another man, temporarily.

Choose a suitable evening and go where you will find others of your own kind, be it pub, club or old school reunion, choose the youngest, best looking and brightest available (and most like husband or partner, if you have any sense) and you do what you can to get yourself pregnant. I have known women do it and I have known it work.

'We're pregnant!' you say, full of pleasure and delight. And your husband's self-esteem is restored, he is spared the indignity of ejaculating into a jar and he loves the baby and never knows. And like as not you'll have another one, because you've relaxed (and because it's inconvenient: babies often come along at the worst possible time, as if nature were bent on challenging you to deny her. When you're ready for the baby, that's when it's least likely to arrive. Nature's little joke, as in the couple with the parrot).

My friend Clara did exactly this, had a boy by a drunken medical student and had three more babies within three years, with her husband, after the first. And now she has grandchildren, and her husband never found out. Just sometimes, when her son, now grown, tells a joke and makes her laugh, she thinks of the student, who might well now be a professor of medicine, and how drunk and funny he was, and wonders what became of him. They might have made something of it, because it was a pleasant encounter, but she didn't follow it up and she loved her husband, even though he never told a joke in his life.

Don't worry about it. Just do it. If you're planning fertility treatment, your need for a child will have overcome your love of your husband in any case.

You're Fertile Enough, But Where's the Man?
Anyone can find a man. It may not be the man you want, but there's a man to be found—at the Job Centre or down the pub. Again, choose as good a genetic specimen as you can. It's a least-worst choice. Babies do not need 'proper' homes. What this baby needs most of all is life. It may say to you from time to time as it grows older, *'I wish I had never been born,'* but it's not likely to mean it. If you can afford a baby, have one.

(If the state has to support it, think again. Giving the child the state for a father is not on. You will need to be mother and father too. If you can do that, good for you.)

Once upon a time men did the hitting and running, planting the gene never to be seen again. Socialization had failed: the man was all-natural unimpeded male. Now you want to hit and run home with the baby. You're all instinct too, and no reason. All nature and no nurture. Socialization has failed but something has been gained: a living, squalling, riotous baby.

240

Let me tell you an historical tale, scarcely relevant to now, but illustrative of the point that what you don't know you don't grieve over. We live in an age of revelation. Manners and mores change fast. Science changes the way we think and feel. We know so much it's hardly possible to work out what's important and what's not. We can get things wrong. If I take you back into the past it's so I myself can get an overview.

This is a true story, set back in the mid-fifties, about a group of college girls seeking truth at a time when nice girls didn't have sex before marriage.

Good Lord, we were ignorant. We lived in a delicious fear that we might be pregnant and then our boyfriends would have to marry us. It wasn't that we lacked sexual experience, it's that the lights were always off and we never *looked*. Or if in the sunlight out of doors, on some grassy romantic sward, we kept our eyes squeezed shut. Men practised the withdrawal method—that is to say, they took their thing out (with any luck) before they finished. At least we thought they did. Our bodies were mysteries to us.

I was to get pregnant very soon and five years later knew pretty much everything about everything—too much for comfort.

241

Men had a 'thing' and we had 'down there'. We sat with our legs crossed as our mothers had taught us.

We were inorgasmic, and in retrospect our dedication to male sexual satisfaction was both absurd and noble. We wanted nothing in return. We were simply grateful to be the object of male attention, and 'dating'—going nearly all the way but not all the way—was exciting enough: the body could be suffused with so much pleasure it was nearly intolerable.

I have no doubt that in other circles in 1950s London there were others who knew about orgasms and even demanded them. There were women who knew everything there was to know. It was just that I and my friends did not.

The day that news of orgasms came to us we were drinking wine in an attic somewhere in Chelsea. None of us were virgins, Elsie, Rowena, Charlotte, Roxy, Brenda and me. We took no notice of our mothers, we loved sex, we wanted sex, we had one-night stands while looking for true love. We were humiliated and distressed when the true love so often left before dawn.

It wasn't much different from *Sex in the City*,

come to that, except the face-saving ritual of the morning-after thank-you call had not yet arrived. Nor, indeed, had safe sex. And abortion was illegal and you went to prison if you had one. We were entranced by the pleasures of the flesh and, believing that sex and procreation were eternally linked, were the more awed by its power. Even if you had an illegitimate baby it was worth it, as I was to find out.

Now we are waiting for Penny to arrive. Penny is our friend, one of our circle. Unlike the rest of us she doesn't have a degree. She has a private income, however, and has gone to see a private doctor about birth control, as it's called. She can afford to. We can't. There's a new thing called a Dutch cap, something that can stop you getting pregnant, and Penny has the courage and means to enquire about it. This is 10 years before the pill and 15 years before the coil and 30 years before implants. No morning-after pills, abortion illegal—no wonder sex was exciting!

We wait impatiently. A Dutch cap! A rubber shield you put over your cervix. *'Where is it?'* *'What's that?'* None of us has a clue. We think Penny is very brave to be prepared to face the embarrassment of an internal examination by a man. (Doctors were normally men.) I'd had one once when I had cystitis, and the doctor, discovering I was not a virgin, sent me off to hospital at once to be tested for venereal disease. My 18-year-old 'down there' was closely inspected by groups of students and declared to be disease-free and I was left to stumble home. It was traumatic but still uninformative.

Roxy, being from Texas, says it's no big deal. Texan girls spend a lot of time with men's hands up their insides as the doctor checks that they are 'developing normally'.

How strange we must have looked by the standards of today: hair in formal waves pulled back unflatteringly from the face, pencilled eyebrows, bright-blue eyeshadow, if any, a general desire to look 40 rather than 20, rubber girdles keeping in our tummies, preventing free movement. Little waists and full skirts. V-necked T-shirts which meant that if you show your shoulders you can't show your cleavage and vice versa.

But they make you feel sexy.

And then in comes Penny, back from the doctor's. She's smiling and she's excited. A revelation has been given to her.

'I had this rubber thing fitted,' says Penny. 'He

says you have to stop everything and put it in, take it out after use and wash it and keep it in a tin. It isn't very romantic.'

The tin was large, flat, round and pink and she showed us the yellowy rubber contraption inside. We were fascinated and horrified.

'I had to lie there on my back with my legs open and he folded the rubber ring and pushed it inside me, where it bounced open. It felt quite nice.'

We were quite shocked. We did not normally go into sexual detail. Penny was less inhibited than the rest of us; she had had less education. She was a girl of the people.

'He was ever so good-looking,' she added, 'and quite young for a doctor. He asked me if I'd ever come. I said, "What's that?" and he said, "Like this." Then he twiddled this little lump in front of down there for a bit and I had this strange feeling, like shivers of electricity all over me, which kind of exploded, and he said, "That's what I mean. It's called an orgasm." "But only men have those," I said. "Women can too," he said. "Now you know, tell your friends."'

And so she did. And Elsie, Rowena, Charlotte, Roxy, Brenda and I pursued orgasms unrelentingly through the coming decades, with varying degrees of success.

Nowadays that doctor would be struck off. We just thought he was useful and a proselytizer for female happiness.

Those of you who can't stand too much attention being paid to the past may rejoin here.

You lot may think we have reached the pinnacle of right thinking, that history is bunk (as Henry Ford said, he who created the gridlocks of the future), that we now know all there is to be known about correct behaviour, but it is not so. Fear of history is denial of history, a burying of the head in the societal sand in case we have to come to terms with what we'd rather not: that everything changes and will forever go on changing, and we are not necessarily going from dark to light, from ignorance to knowledge, from barbarism to civilization.

The ostrich with its head in the sand is not happy, just fearful.

Now you shall have a final parable, the parable of Sylvia the housewife, who, when the four horsemen circled nearer, their nags champing and snorting, managed calmly and quietly to send them packing, while scarcely knowing she was doing it. She is the nearest person to a saint that I have ever met.

Mrs Blackbird

In the twenty-two years they had called the place home the suburbs had been raised around them. Now, when asked, Sylvia hardly knew whether to say 'I live in the country' or 'I live in the town.' Two years back, just before the divorce, Hugh had done a deal by which the acre field which went with the house had been sold off for development. Now Sylvia was overlooked by neighbours. They were pleasant enough and she could see she was lucky and what garden remained was large by their standards, but there were street lights all around and she missed the dark of a night which made the stars seem bright and important and her place in the universe, though humble, made clear. Namely, that she was needed in the great scheme of things, if only as an observer. Humanity, in Sylvia's opinion, existed to glorify its creator.

When she'd said this kind of thing to Hugh he'd been embarrassed, and she thought it was one of the reasons that he had left her— very amiably, and politely, and leaving her well enough provided for, and visiting quite often, but still he had left, for a nice bright rational young woman, Debbie, who saw no sub-text in life at all and never had irritating fits of whimsy. Sylvia liked to exchange ideas; other people, it seemed, including Hugh, preferred to trade information.

The new neighbours didn't go for Sylvia's kind of conversation either. They walked their dogs and said, 'Lovely evening,' and a few sat on riverbanks and pretended to be fishing, but mostly they talked about home improvements if they were men and diets if they were women, and the whys and wherefores of their existence didn't seem to worry them at all.

The new houses were little better than boxes, computer designed to make the best use of every square inch of space at the lowest possible price. Sylvia and Hugh's old farmhouse, with its lack of right angles and wandering corridors, was the one which now seemed out of place. And now Hugh was no longer there Sylvia could see herself increasingly cast as an oddity, a woman of a certain age, without a family, cut off from friends. Once she had been envied; now she was pitied.

Since Hugh had taken to property

development he'd grown rich, spurred on by the realization that you could build a house for £15,000 and sell it for £250,000. He'd grown rather fat and dull too, but was still quite a catch, apparently, for Debbie. Debbie could have babies, which Sylvia couldn't any more, having lost the one she'd had and messed up her insides, so Hugh was scarcely to be blamed for leaving. Why should her life's affliction become his, just because they were married? When he left she just felt blank. Now, a couple of years later, she could hardly think of a thing to say to him. She seldom had much to report.

Yes, she was fine, she had rejoined the library and was working on the garden, and no, she didn't want a holiday, and certainly not a cruise, not even if he and the pregnant Debbie came too. And then what was there to say? Hugh was not interested in the fate of the swallows which had gone elsewhere when their barn was destroyed to make way for the bungalow, or how the robin had weathered the winter. He did not care that Mrs Blackbird, who had fled when the ivy where she nested had been showered with lime and plaster dust, had returned after a season's absence and had set up home in the Virginia creeper outside Sylvia's bedroom window. She tried to tell him, but Hugh sounded puzzled and asked her how on earth she knew it was the same bird as before. When she came to think of it, of course she did not. She just hoped it was. So she shut up.

Sylvia was prone to wishful thinking: she knew she was. She had really believed that Hugh and Debbie were just good friends. All the same, she was home to a blackbird. She woke to her song every morning. She liked to think the bird knew the difference between her and the incomers, and preferred her, and included her in her singing. 'Oh, what a beautiful morning!'

She must not get too fond of Mrs Blackbird, though, the little boy in the new house next door pointed out, peering up at her with his plump, anxious, small-eyed little face, since the bird was marked for doom.

The boy's name was Darren. Sylvia supposed he was 9 or 10. She did not know much about children.

'What do you mean, marked out for doom?' Sylvia asked, crossly. She was snipping out extra buds from the roses—snip, snip, snip— to ensure extra good blooms later on. It was a wonderful sunny May that year.

'Our cat will get it,' Darren said.

'I certainly hope not,' she said.

'A cat's got to eat,' he said. 'That's nature, isn't it?'

'Then keep yours well fed,' she said, briskly, 'and don't let me see it in my garden.'

'You're weird,' he said and wandered off.

She felt she had exchanged Hugh for this grungy little boy called Darren Croxton. It had not been a good bargain. His eyes were too narrow and anxious, too close together, and his skin was grey: a slum child by breeding. Her little girl, had she lived beyond two days, would have been on the side of the angels, and not spoken to her in that way. Yet she could see this wretched boy, by virtue of living in what had once been her orchard, was in some way her responsibility.

It was true there were now too many cats in the neighbourhood for the safety of Mrs Blackbird. There was a slinky Burmese called Khan, who prowled around meaningfully but fortunately did not seem to have the energy to pounce. There was an amazing creature called Catso by its owner, a good-looking young man with a Lamborghini and male friends—a Bengal cat who lived across the way, had tiger markings on its belly and was five generations down from a miniature Bengal tiger, bred for its good nature. So successfully had it been bred, indeed, that it seemed to love everyone and everything, gazing indulgently at flies and wishing even small birds like Mrs Blackbird well. It had cost £2,000 and was electronically tagged, like a criminal. It would come and sit by Sylvia's side down where the parsley and the sage grew, and they'd listen to Mrs Blackbird together, and Catso would even purr.

The cat Sylvia feared was the black-and-white tom Henry, from the Croxtons' house next door. Henry, as you might expect from such a household, was a miserable, uncared-for specimen, scrawny, with a savage gleam in his eye, whose pleasure was catching birds and laying them out on the garden path. He would sit and stare up at Mrs Blackbird's nest in the Virginia creeper. As Darren had observed, it was only natural for cats to want to kill birds, but Sylvia did not want it to happen.

The day after the Croxtons moved in Sylvia discovered Darren in her herb patch, picking parsley. He wanted his mother to make him a parsley omelette. It was evident from what the child said that he did not know the difference between a field, a common and a private garden, and also that his feckless

252

mother scarcely owned a frying pan. They lived on takeaways. So Sylvia made him a parsley omelette and he said it tasted weird—his favourite word—but he ate most of it, spitting out the parsley into his hand. He hadn't realized it was so green. He did not like green food.

The Croxtons came from the inner city and had moved out, people said disapprovingly, not so much in search of fresh air as profit. Stay in one of the new developments for a year, make a few 'improvements' and you could sell on with a good mark-up, while in the meantime avoiding the pain of paid employment.

Now Darren seemed to be round at Sylvia's place all the time, his little anxious malnourished face appearing without warning, almost out from under her arm as it were, asking questions and making demands—a glass of water here, a plaster there, a piece of cake, would she look after his key in case he lost it? His parents never heard when he knocked. They smoked a lot of stuff, he explained, and kept the doors locked, but she wasn't to tell anyone. It was a question of the law.

'Do your parents mind me having the key?' she'd asked, ckecking.

'Nah,' he said. 'They say you're an old bat but you're okay.'

She took the key, not without reluctance, well aware that for every favour you granted more would be asked and less gratitude felt. The parents could barely be in their thirties. They must have started out in their teens with Darren. Of course they would think she was an old bat. If Sylvia had bothered to have the grey taken out of her hair and wore something other than flat shoes, elasticized skirts and old jumpers around the house she could have looked as good as Debbie, just older. She had better features than Debbie and a nicer nature than Debbie, which was why Hugh was always coming round, but she could see that to the outside world she could very well be an old bat. The barn had been converted to a nifty home for a Bengal cat and the real bats had fled, but that was the way of the new world. Perhaps they had left some of the spirit of battedness behind and it had lodged in her. That was okay by Sylvia.

No one thought much of the Croxtons. They let the side down, they didn't belong to this smart new development any more than Sylvia did. The father spent his time putting in patterned glass doors instead of plain, decking the garden and sticking pink plastic flamingos in what grass was left. Family rows could be heard down the street and the mother had been seen at the benefits office. She could see the blue-grey glow from the computer in Darren's bedroom late into the night, sometimes at three in the morning. She could take a broom and tap on his window and tell him to go to bed at once, but it was none of her business. In the morning he'd leave at a run for school, often late, eating some chocolate bar as he ran.

She took to leaving a plate of premium cat food for Henry under the apple tree to keep him well fed, smarten up his coat a bit and keep him away from Mrs Blackbird. Mr Blackbird, shiny and glossy and grand, appeared from time to time now that Mrs Blackbird had done all the work building a neat, well-hidden nest from twigs and moss, mud and leaves. He'd put his head on one side and add the odd well-placed twig. He reminded her of Hugh.

Mrs Blackbird laid her eggs and Henry prowled nearer and nearer.

'They won't make it,' Darren said. 'One in three fledgling thrushes don't.' He'd looked it up on the Internet. 'If it's not the cats, it's the rats and the squirrels. And the crows eat the eggs. And my mum says you're trying to steal her cat. She says if you don't stop feeding it she'll beat the shit out of you.'

Sylvia raised surprised eyebrows at Darren, who amended it to, weakly: 'Mum says would you please not do it.' She called round at Mrs Croxton's and though she was pretty sure the woman was in there, no one came to the door. So she went on putting food out for Henry under the apple tree. If Darren's mother had something to say to her, let her come round and say it.

Then Darren didn't come round for a time, until the fledglings had learned to fly and had left the nest. She imagined he was sulking about the cat food and punishing her. That was okay by her. Then she found him digging up her lawn with a spoon and putting in half-live worms he'd dug out of his own pitiful garden. He said he was providing extra food for Mrs Blackbird, but Sylvia suspected he was trying to lure the bird back onto the open lawn so Henry could do his pouncing. She said as much to Darren, who shouted and shrieked and swore, so she knew he was guilty. Really, he was a wretched child. He kept out of her way for a week or so. Good.

Then she saw a removal van draw up next door and the men load on the Croxtons' household belongings which were not up to much. Darren had gone off to school as usual. Into the van went a big plasma-screen TV, Darren's computer and a rather smart bath, amongst the barely serviceable rubbish of next door's everyday life.

Mrs Croxton came out and lured Henry into a cat box from under the apple tree, casting a snarling glance over towards Sylvia's house, while Mr Croxton removed all the light bulbs from the rooms and the fittings from the front door, and off they all went.

Later that day a bright-looking young couple turned up at the door and let themselves in and Sylvia heard cries of dismay and angry phone calls being made, and soon bin bag after bin bag of assorted debris and dirt started piling up at the gate. And Darren hadn't even called to say goodbye. She was more hurt than she had expected. A horrid lad, really.

But then there he was at her door again, in floods of tears, beside himself, and the new people next door were with him and asking her what to do, as if she were expected to know. The child had come home from school and found his parents gone.

'They took Henry,' he was saying, 'They left

me!' And so it seemed the parents had. Flown the nest and left the fledgling.

'I know I'm bad,' he wept, 'but not as bad as all that.'

Social services said it did sometimes happen to children, just as it happened to dogs. The owners get fed up and scarper.

'I'm sorry about the worms,' said Darren. 'I didn't mean it. I really like Mrs Blackbird. I just wanted to know what happened next.'

'It's all right, all right,' she said, and found him an apple from Henry's tree, but when social services suggested that Darren stayed with her while they sorted things out and that she could even foster him if she passed the tests, she refused. She was too old, she had no intention of taking on a child, she knew nothing about children, she'd never had one, or one that lasted.

'You're just weird,' Darren shrieked at her. 'You are not too old, you just say you are. I hate you!' They dragged him off her, bribed him with a chocolate bar and took him away in their car to a fate in care.

The next day Sylvia was sitting in the garden when a mother crow alighted on the garden wall, followed by two fluttering baby crows. The three of them sat on the wall, the big bird impatient and cross, as crows always seem to be, the little ones unsleek and bumbling and rendered unnaturally large by virtue of having fluff rather than feather.

Mother Crow flew down from the wall to the garden. The babies were meant to follow. They wouldn't. They peered, they craned, they saw unimaginable depths below and refused to take the risk. They shook their heads. Up flew Mother Crow and tried again. Still they refused. Then Mrs Blackbird came and sat beside the three of them and watched. Crows and blackbirds do not normally get on. Blackbirds keep out of crows' way if they can. But Mrs Blackbird seemed to have forgotten caution.

Three more times Mother Crow gave her tutorial. 'This is the wall. This is the ground. Now fly from one to the other.' It was so simple for her. Three times more the babies looked at her and then at each other and shook their heads. Mother Crow, fed up, took off to a tall ash tree and sulked.

Mother Blackbird took on her job. She fluttered down from the wall to the garden. The babies looked on curiously. Two more times she did it and then one of the baby

259

crows launched into space and joined her on the ground. The other one followed. Mrs Blackbird flew back up. The babies fluttered up after her. Mother Blackbird took a short flight, the baby crows followed. All returned to their wall and sat there, preening and proud. She'd taught, they'd learned, all had done as nature required.

Mother Crow flew back from her high ash branch. They were her children, after all. Mrs Blackbird prudently flew off. Mr Blackbird set up a terrible squawking.

And Sylvia, Sylvia went to the phone and called social services and said she'd look after Darren until other arrangements could be made, knowing full well that as long as she was on tap they'd probably not get round to 'other'. Darren would be with her for good. But a child is a child, and needs to be taught, and teaching the young is in the blood (unless you're the Croxtons), and anyone can do it. Crow, blackbird, human, so what? Hugh wouldn't think much of it, he'd squawk away, but he wasn't really much to do with Sylvia any more, and she'd have a new household.

Moral

If a blackbird can do it in the face
of a crow, so can you.

Something Here Inside

It's the reason most people go to therapists—something inside that torments them, a prisoner waiting be unlocked. You don't quite know where she is, you don't know quite what she's done, but she's there. *'Please, please, please,'* she's crying, *'let me out.'*

Desperate to help, you look for answers. You wonder, *'Is it my inner rage, my lack of self-assertiveness, something terrible that happened in my childhood? My father or my mother, current spouse, passing partner?'*

A therapist can steer you off in one direction or another and stop you washing your hands ten times in ten minutes, or losing all your friends by your cruel frankness (*'It's the truth, so you need to know it'*). But the feeling of something even less specific and more distressing that there is something terribly wrong can remain. You feel you have to get out of this relationship or die. The prisoner within is making too much racket. Not even the therapist can deafen you to her cries.

That's when a woman absconds from a perfectly good relationship, or throws out perfectly reasonable lovers and tries others. She's desperate. No-one understands but she'll have to put up with that.

Personally, I never had much difficulty in releasing the inner me, inasmuch as I cried copiously through my adolescence and early marriages without even the benefit of a therapist. I released all over the place and messed up my life, and that of others, self-esteem rock bottom, falling into the wrong beds, all that.

My problem was getting the prisoner back *inside*, locking her up, and I finally did it with the help of a stern and rigorous Freudian psychoanalyst. It only then became apparent that I'd got the wrong prisoner. There were two of them. The destructive one was in there, properly locked up, and just as well, at least for the time being, but actually there was someone in the next cell down, someone wholly innocent, not allowing me to live in peace.

My poor wretched bleeding soul was still waiting to be released, desperate for a little attention before she shrivelled up altogether. She didn't want to leave, she just wanted the door unlocked so she could wander round.

The very act of acknowledgement allowed the

poor trapped thing out of there.

There are three parts of you. There is the body and its instincts (nature), there is the brain and its machinations (nurture) and there is the soul (God given).

Many, nervous of such a definition because it sounds so soppy and they are of a scientific bent, and where would you physically locate this thing anyway, link brain and soul together and refer to that as a third thing called 'mind'. That seems to me to be a cowardly approach.

Philosophers of the 'mind' do get as far as referring to the 'doxastic' state of the mind—that is, the awareness of 'belief'—and to 'non-doxastic' states—the awareness of information or emotion being processed—and separate out the two, and that's fine. Then what I had wrongly shut up inside was a doxastic state. It still needed to be released in order to make sense of the whole. *'Come on out, Doxastic! Welcome.'*

The marvel is that we are here on this Earth at all. Take a moment to think about it. A sense of wonder at our very existence, at the complexity and interaction of mind, body and soul is in itself healing. I know it's difficult. Depression can make you blind to the overall scheme of things, deaf to the music of the spheres. But small ridiculous things can open your eyes and ears. Pictures from Hubble, an aria by Mozart caught on the radio as you switch from one station to another, a landscape as you fight the traffic on the motorway—clues are given and are God sent. Personally, I go to church and sing old hymns. That does it.

The voice of the prisoner inside stops clamouring. She's okay. You are happy in yourself. You are no longer self-obsessed, trapped in your anxious, guilty, instinct-ridden body, looking for solace in transitory sensual solutions. You are a whole.

And that is why I say, *'Be good and you'll be happy. Be happy and you'll be good.'* These are the words that set the prisoner free.

Notes on the Soul

When I was a small child in New Zealand and going to a convent school, there was nothing but. Souls had to be kept pure and untarnished, and were always in danger from the devil, who tried to steal them. But they could be sold to him in an emergency. The body was the temple of the soul, which was why you had to keep it clean and in order and not mess about with it, in honour of what was inside you. (Which is why today I have a dislike of face painting on children, body piercing and so on, yet don't object to cosmetic surgery, that being building work on the temple, and decorative.)

I had the idea that our souls hovered over our heads like the proud milky little cloud in Pooh Bear, tethered by a golden cord and rather talkative. I asked the nuns and they said no, souls were inside us, and silent, and I asked where, and they pointed variously to the heart or just above the bridge of the nose.

I thought then perhaps souls were like the white inner sole of a slipper—they would have to be very thin and flexible to fit in. But I was told, no, every soul was different and none of this really mattered, the important thing was to treasure your soul and keep it from harm, or else you went to hell—or if you were me, and unchristened—to a place called Limbo. And if I didn't stop asking questions, such was the implication, I'd be there quicker than I imagined.

But I believed the nuns and I still do. The soul is the essential part of us, the inner recognizable core which stays the same while the body which ties us down changes. We blossom and flourish, like leaves on the tree, and wither and perish, but our souls go marching on, at least if we have in our lives allowed ourselves enough exhilaration, enough elation, enough wonder at the marvel of creation to keep ourselves spiritually sustained and the four horsemen at bay.